DREAM DESIGN DO
FROM BROKE TO $3MILLION IN PROPERTY IN 2 YEARS
BY ZAKI AMEER

Dream, Design, Do
First published in 2014
CreateSpace
P.O. Box 81226
Seattle, WA 98108

This book is copyright. Apart from any fair dealing for the purpose of private study, research criticism or review, as permitted under the Copyright Act 1988, no part of this publication may be reproduced by any process or by any means, electronic, photocopied, recorded or otherwise without permission of the copyright owner. Enquiries for reproduction should be addressed to Zaki Ameer.

ISBN-13: 9781503138711

Copyright 2014 Zaki Ameer

Disclaimer: Any financial and legal advice offered by the author of this book is of a general nature and may not be suitable for some people. No individual financial or legal needs or goals have been taken into account in the advice offered; you should always seek independent advice about specific financial and legal decisions. The author of this book disclaims all and any responsibility or liability in respect of information detailed or omitted (or the consequences thereof) from this book or any other meetings held with the author.

This book is not intended to provide personalised legal, financial, or investment advice. The authors and the published disclaim any liability, loss or risk which is incurred as a consequence, directly or indirectly, of

DREAM, DESIGN, DO

*Dedicated to mum and dad for being
pillars of strength and spirit.*

DREAM, DESIGN, DO

INTRODUCTION

DREAM!

Everything great that has ever been created or accomplished started with a dream. Landing on the moon, sending a rocket into space, circumnavigating the world, climbing Mt Everest for the first time ... these all began as dreams.

Basic things that we take for granted today like books and the internet and running water first began as dreams. The café you recently went to and the coffee you drank there, they all started as somebody's dream.

You have dreams of your own too, but maybe you've dismissed them or just never acted on them. I want to let you know that it's OK to dream. While reading this book I want you to give yourself permission to dream. Ask yourself now – what is your dream?

DESIGN!

But whatever your dream is, merely having it won't get you there. If you never do anything, your dream will remain just that, a dream, and nothing more.

In order to make your dream a reality you need to have a strategy. A strategy is a series of planned actions focused on bringing your dream to life. Mahatma Gandhi had the dream of Indian self-rule and removing the British that governed India at the time. His strategy to achieve that was passive non-violence. The United States had the dream to land people on moon. Their strategy was to build a rocket that could launch into space and safely return to earth.

Having a strategy is crucial in translating dreams into reality. Without a strategy there are no clear steps about how to achieve your dream. A strategy is something you want to develop.

DO!

This is the exciting part! This is where it gets real. You have your dream and you have your strategy. But without the doing, the dream remains a dream and what's the point in that?

When you talk, but don't do, you feel bad about yourself and you begin to doubt whether your dream will ever happen. This is what psychologists call 'cognitive dissonance'. The opposite holds true as well. When you dream and take the steps to make it a reality you feel great about yourself. Progress may be slow, but you know you're headed in the right direction.

All men dream, but not equally. Those who dream by night in the dusty recesses of their minds, wake in the day to find it was vanity: but the dreamers of the day are dangerous men, for they may act on their dreams with open eyes, to make them possible.

T. E. Lawrence
(commonly known as Lawrence of Arabia)

IN SHORTER WORDS – DREAM, DESIGN, DO!

This book is about a dream I had and the strategy I undertook to make it happen. A strategy that allowed me to build a portfolio of ten properties in two years.

When someone talks about property how do you feel? Nervous? Unsure? A little bit overwhelmed and lost about where to start?

If you feel any of this it's pretty normal. Any discussion that touches on personal finance and investing is an emotionally loaded topic for many people.

I believe that people avoid investing in property, or make bad investment decisions, because they lack self-belief and a clear, simple, proven strategy to follow. This book is about sharing that strategy with you and giving you the self-belief to make it happen.

I'm going to make things very simple and relatable. Albert Einstein once said **'Everything should be made as simple as possible but not simpler'**. That is what will happen here.

I'm writing this book for the first-time investor that wants to get into the game but doesn't know how. (Seasoned investors who began investing before they could talk are best directed elsewhere.)

Once you've finished this book, you'll walk away with motivation, clarity and understanding as to how you can begin your property investing journey. From this place, you'll be able take action and do what you have to do so that you can live a life of financial abundance.

Zaki Ameer
November 2013

DREAM, DESIGN, DO

CONTENTS

CHAPTER 1: MY STORY — 11
Where I am now and how I got to be here.

CHAPTER 2: WHY DO YOU WANT TO INVEST? — 25
Understanding the why before you begin will propel you forward and keep you going.

CHAPTER 3: STRATEGIES THAT IT'S BEST YOU DON'T USE — 33
Here I lay out the strategies that don't often lead to the financial independence you want.

CHAPTER 4: THE STRATEGY I USED TO BUY 10 PROPERTIES IN 3 YEARS — 43
The strategy that worked for me, and why it worked.

CHAPTER 5: FINANCE — 53
The details around the money you use to make it all happen.

CHAPTER 6: RENOVATIONS — 67
How to add value to a house on time and on budget (and not lose your hair).

CHAPTER 7: REPEATING THE PROCESS — 75
How to win ... again and again.

CHAPTER 8: LEARNING FROM THOSE WHO'VE SUCCEEDED BEFORE YOU — 83
Resources to help you win in all areas of life.

This is the road map we'll be following.
Now let's get into it!

DREAM, DESIGN, DO

CHAPTER 1:
MY STORY

When you pick up property investing magazines you'll often see sensationalist headlines like *'Rags to Riches!!!'* That's what people like to read in such publications.

It's true; I've had my story featured in articles just like that.

But what often goes unmentioned is that *'Rags to Riches'* isn't the whole of it. In truth my story actually starts out as *'Riches to Rags'*.

I was born in Sri Lanka in 1979 into a wealthy and loving family. My grandfather created and started his own shoe company, building it into a firm known and loved across the island. Later my father did exactly the same thing, creating *his* own shoe company that became known and loved across the country as well.

Family life was an environment of warmth and love for me, my brother and sister. All of our needs were met. There were maids and servants looking after us. There were constant feasts and celebrations. We lacked for nothing.

I was a mischievous troublemaker. One particular incident I remember very clearly was when I convinced the photocopy guy at school to photocopy my exam papers for me. All hell would've descended if I was found out. I only gave him fifty dollars too.

My father was from the old school. He demanded respect and obedience. It didn't matter if we were mischievous or didn't get the best grades, as long as we did what we were told. Something he valued very highly was education – so he sent us to the very best school in Sri Lanka.

Colombo International School was where the top one percent

or a car company. My immediate family wasn't that wealthy in comparison so I kind of felt like an outcast. But not in a bad way. Most of my friends came from inherited wealth, so they had a real sense of entitlement and weren't particularly entrepreneurial. My mindset was a little different.

My father was the person I modeled myself on. Growing up, I saw him start his own company and persist in the face of setbacks until he succeeded. Originally my father had part ownership in my grandfather's business but after a family disagreement he lost it all and had to start again from scratch. Watching him build his wealth again to a level even higher than the original family business taught me that I would always be able to stand on my own two feet.

Entrance to the Colombo International School required a deposit equivalent to $200,000 in today's money. It was a lot for my dad – it's a lot for anyone really! Yet he found a way to make it happen. I learnt from him that you can always find a way to do what you need to. Education was something he really valued as he knew that if you educate your children they will be ahead in life. You can take everything away from someone but you can't take what's in their mind. Consider Bill Gates. If you strip him of everything he will quickly build it all back up again because of his mindset and experiences.

While I received a good education at a very good school I wasn't academic at all. My marks were always D's, E's and F's. For me school was all about fun. I'd play pranks. I ran little businesses on the side. I didn't take things too seriously and was always the one organising the parties. Although my father was disappointed by my bad academic record it wasn't crucial to him. Maybe it was because he wasn't academic. The freedom that he gave me was the chance to dream big. I was free to think of ideas and do them, while my school friends just studied. If they didn't get A's they'd be in trouble.

But all things must come to an end. I entered school aged three, and at eighteen it was time to move on. Colombo International was a private English school run by teachers from England, so the

study at Oxford or Cambridge. A few went to Yale and Stanford in the United States. Then there were the oddballs like me that decided to go to Australia.

AUSTRALIA

I arrived at Sydney International Airport at the end of 1998. I was extremely excited and a little nervous as I wheeled my suitcase along. It was a bit of a risk coming to Australia. If I had gone to the States or the UK, I'd have had a bigger support network, with more friends and family contacts – yet here I was on my own.

Despite all the logical reasons not to come, I had an inner calling to go to Australia. Sometimes you just get an idea in your mind you have to act on. I was excited at the new life that was opening up before me. This was Sydney! Bondi Beach, the Opera House, the Harbour Bridge … these were all the images I had in mind of Sydney and I was looking forward to exploring them.

Shortly after arriving and settling down I enrolled at the University of Sydney to study a Bachelor of Engineering. Please don't ask me why I did so. I still don't know why! I think I did it because that's what all my other friends from school went on to study – or that in Sri Lanka it was the sexy and popular thing to do. I set myself up in a nice little studio apartment a few minutes walk away from the campus, dutifully bought all the textbooks the subject outlines told me to buy and awaited my first class.

After a few lectures I quickly learnt that engineering was not for me. I was learning about maths and physics and a whole lot of other stuff that I really didn't care about. Sitting in lecture theatres listening to theories that meant nothing to me was extremely frustrating and aggravating. I was completely out of my zone.

I just wanted to be in the outside world, where deals were being done and to do deals of my own.

Growing up as a teen I loved doing deals. When I was thirteen I remember selling cassettes to people at school. I'd record the top

lot of fun. But soon that became too easy. I wanted to do more! So I organised huge parties. I'd find a warehouse, or some empty building, then find DJs. Next step was getting people to the party. I'd promote it hard with posters and word of mouth. Tickets sold fast, and every few weekends the teenagers of Colombo would be treated to the best party of their lives. Of course, I made money from all these little ventures, which was a bonus.

When I share these stories, people are often curious and ask what it felt like making money. For me at that time, and to this day, it wasn't about making money. It was more about the fun and the joy of making deals, of being the middleman who brought people together and got a cut or commission for doing so. I call it 'connecting dots' and that's what I continue to do to this day.

But back in the University of Sydney lecture theatre I wasn't connecting any dots – at least not in the ways that I wanted to. An uncomfortable realisation was dawning that I didn't want to study engineering and that my future wasn't there. The realisation was uncomfortable because my dad was paying a lot of money for me to be in Australia. There was the tuition of $25,000 a year. Then there was the $350 rent a week he was paying for my little studio apartment. Then there was the money he was giving me to cover my living expenses, and my weekly allowance so that I could enjoy myself. I began to feel really bad. I was very conflicted. It wasn't like I could easily switch course either – the premise of my student visa was based on me studying engineering. I'd speak to my dad and mum on the phone and say stuff like 'Everything's good! I love it here!', then hang up the receiver feeling guilty. I wished I'd never heard of engineering.

The universe must have heard my wish. One day I was on the phone with my family and they told me that my father had run into problems with his business. As a result they wouldn't be able to support me as much anymore. It's not like they cut support completely and straight away – it was a gradual thing. Financial support from my parents was $600 a week, then it became $300, then $100, then finally it became zero. At that point I was told that I could come home and they'd support me, but if I decided to stay

I stuck to my guns and told them I was staying in Australia. In my mind my parents had betrayed me and the idea of going back home was reprehensible. Home didn't exist anymore and I had a keen sense of anger towards them. I certainly held onto that disappointment and anger for quite a few years.

My life quickly changed after that decision. It's one thing not knowing anyone, not knowing the country, its culture, or how it works, yet still having money. If you have money you can survive financially. But if you don't have money, you become a homeless person with no idea where you belong. That's what happened to me. I found myself locked out of the studio apartment when I wasn't able to pay the rent.

Instead, I quickly found a house with a granny flat to move into. There were other things I had to address too. I was going to have to work full time to support myself – but I had to study as well.

Remember I said that the universe must have been listening to me? Well, I wasn't to study engineering anymore. These events gave me the chance to change my course. In order to work full time I had to study in the evenings. The only university that offered full-time study in the evenings was the University of Western Sydney. I quickly and enthusiastically dropped my engineering degree and replaced it with a Bachelor of Business, something much closer to the deal-making I wanted to be doing.

Finding work was the next step. These were the days before online job boards so I bought the paper every day and applied to all the positions advertised. I must have gone to about ten interviews, but I had no luck, nothing was happening.

'Why don't you work at our friend's fruit shop?', my host family even offered.

'Fruit shop!?', I thought. No way! I just couldn't handle the idea of that.

Fortunately one day I found myself sitting across from an

a data entry job paying $16 an hour in Circular Quay. I was very excited. I'd never had a job so I was looking forward to the new experience and proving to myself that I could make my own way. I'd also earn $600 a week, which for me was pretty good money, enough to cover all my essentials.

All this time I was like a nomad. I moved out of the granny flat and then six times from house to house, into rooms smaller than prison cells. Rent was $90 a week – that's how much my budget allowed and that's why the rooms I lived in were so small. I was surrounded by negative people in very weird and depressing areas. Imagine all of the people you never want to meet or associate with: alcoholics, junkies, people with anger management issues. That was who I was surrounded by. The people that lived in these environments were either divorced or in destructive relationships. It wasn't a place of hope. It wasn't a place you went to be uplifted and have your spirit revitalised. The air was heavy with depression and desperation. It was draining and suffocating.

It was like being reborn as a child into a completely different environment. Sometimes I caught myself thinking, **'OK. When am I going to wake up? When am I going to escape this nightmare?'**

Every morning I'd bravely put on my shirt, my suit, shoes and tie. It was my armour. It's how I differentiated myself from everyone I lived with. I'd leave the environment I called 'home' and catch the bus and train into Circular Quay, where I'd work eight hours from nine to five. At work I'd keep to myself. I really was like an alien. I didn't know how to talk to people. I knew how to speak English but I never understood the slang or the culture. Many times people would say something to me and I'd mistakenly think they had insulted me – I never understood sarcasm. So there I'd be at work feeling insulted and further losing my confidence. Back then I didn't have the self-belief or confidence I have now.

But come five o'clock my day wasn't over. Not by a long shot. From Circular Quay it would take me ninety minutes to get to the university in Campbelltown where, battling mental exhaustion, I'd force myself to stay awake long enough to listen to the lecturer

any assignments or upcoming exams to study for I'd quickly fall asleep. If there were upcoming exams or assignment work it was no sleep for me. That was my life, Monday to Friday, for four years. It was a grueling and monotonous cycle.

I call these days my 'dark ages'. It was just a horrible, horrible time that stretched me emotionally, mentally and physically. These days I may have a dark day but I know I'll come out the other side OK. Back then I just felt hopeless, like I was in a black pit with no light to be seen.

People tell me that I must have been very brave and determined to stay in Australia given all the setbacks I had. They say that at any time I could have returned to Sri Lanka. All my friends and family would be there and life would be smooth sailing and comfortable again.

If I saw that as an option I probably would have taken it. But in my mind my family had deserted me. **'Home', my family in Sri Lanka and the world I came from, didn't exist for me anymore.** The bridge behind me had disappeared and my foundation of support had vanished. I had no choice – I had to keep going. If I relented I'd have been *sent* back home. I didn't even have the option of being homeless.

Through all of that I just kept going. It reminds me of this poem:

INVICTUS BY WILLIAM ERNEST HENLEY

Out of the night that covers me,

Black as the Pit from pole to pole,

I thank whatever gods may be

For my unconquerable soul.

In the fell clutch of circumstance

I have not winced nor cried aloud.

Under the bludgeoning of chance

DREAM, DESIGN, DO

> *Beyond this place of wrath and tears*
> *Looms but the Horror of the shade,*
> *And yet the menace of the years*
> *Finds, and shall find, me unafraid.*
> *It matters not how strait the gate,*
> *How charged with punishments the scroll.*
> *I am the master of my fate:*
> *I am the captain of my soul.*

That poem is such an encouragement. Life was beating me up at the time but rather obstinately I stuck around. The only plan I had was to get permanent residency. I didn't want to leave the country without it.

I was failing university however. For the first one-and-a-half years it was just fail, fail, fail. A fail for every subject. I was really depressed at that time, except I didn't recognise it as depression. Back home in Sri Lanka those things were never spoken about. I didn't know what I didn't know, and thus could never treat my depression or get help.

One day I did get a kick up the pants which made me spring into action and forget all my woes and misery. Immigration told me that if I were to fail just one more subject I wouldn't be allowed to stay in the country. From that I summoned the inner drive to find the time to study so I could at least pass.

Reading all of this you could be forgiven for thinking that my life was complete misery. That's not the entire truth. I learnt to make do in every situation and to enjoy what I had. At work I made it my purpose to do a great job and I enjoyed working. In my fifteen years of full-time work I was promoted six times, and gradually I learnt to socialise and get along well with everyone.

I made a lot of Sri Lankan friends and we'd travel around the countryside on weekends. I'd leave Sydney in a hire car on a Friday night and return on Sunday night. That way I was able to travel around much of Australia and have a good time. To this day I still love to drive – it's like a form of meditation to me. Sitting in the driver's seat, being in control of the car, feeling the responsiveness of the machine on the road and watching beautiful scenery pass by; it's very relaxing for me. At that time it was my outlet, the place where I could forget about my troubles.

I eventually passed university. It took me five years to complete a three-year course. I graduated from the University of Western Sydney with a Bachelor of Business in Information Systems. Six months after graduating I got my permanent residency, which was an amazing feeling. It was a feeling of deep peace and accomplishment. Despite the struggle and personal toll it took me to get there, the fact was I did it. I put in the effort and finally it was all over. I could relax a bit.

From there I got my first permanent job with St. George Bank. Before I only had done temporary work organised through agencies. Here was my first permanent job, where I worked in loan administration earning $17.50 an hour.

With my new job and my studies over I was able to move out of the prison-cell share house and into a two-bedroom apartment with a flatmate. It was paradise.

THE DOOR-TO-DOOR SALESMAN

In 2004, shortly after starting work with St. George, something amazing happened – an experience that was set to change my life.

I was at a family friend's wedding and I met someone who said, 'You have to come to this seminar!' To this day I'm very grateful to that person for saying that. Some people call these occurrences 'the angel', 'the game changer', or just the dots you connect after the event has happened. People walk into your life for a reason and you only know the reason when you take the opportunity.

This seminar was the first time I was introduced to an environment where people came to be inspired. At the time the only role models I had were my family and my dad. This was the first time I'd entered a bigger environment, where the person on stage was the inspiration. I was mesmerised, as what I heard and the conversations I was having with people were a match with all that I'd learnt at home from my dad. He taught me a great deal. He instilled the conversations and philosophies of business in me every day. He'd talk about all that was on his mind – the success, the daily challenges of running a business. I learnt a great deal just by listening. He also taught me the value of dressing well and looking good no matter what, regardless of how you were feeling. That you can never be overeducated or overdressed (Oscar Wilde said that) are still things I remember from my father to this day. He was also generous. One day, out of the blue, he gave me 500 rupees, the equivalent of $5, which was a lot of money for me. I hadn't done anything special to merit this reward, and that gesture has stayed with me. From that I learnt that you don't only reward people when they've done something remarkable. It's also important to thank and reward them when they're doing their job or meeting their responsibilities. He also taught me to always be grateful, thankful and appreciative of what you have, and this was what I was now hearing at this seminar.

That seminar was the beginning of my journey in personal development. From there on every day without fail I would read autobiographies of great people, as well as self-help classics like **How to Win Friends and Influence People** by Dale Carnegie, **The Magic of Thinking Big** by Daniel Schwartz and **Think and Grow Rich** by Napoleon Hill. I made sure to attend at least one personal development seminar a week to keep my mind fresh with inspiration, as well as to meet new, quality people.

It was through these seminars and programs that I was introduced to a direct-selling business that sold water- and air-purification systems. I was at a stage in my life where I was open to something new. I wanted to challenge and push myself and put into practice everything I'd read in my personal development books. It also helped that I loved the products (and still use them).

As a door-to-door salesman every evening for four years I'd walk the streets, knock on doors, go into people's houses, do presentations and sell the product.

I could have continued to work at St. George and just worked nine to five like everyone else. But ever since I was a kid I was always doing something on the side. Selling music tapes. Organising parties. When studying I worked full time, so now this was the next thing for me. It reminds me of the phrase **'the beggar and the wealthy have the same twenty-four hours in a day'**. What you do with those hours is the difference in the outcome of your life.

When I first started I sucked at selling. I really did. However, I committed to getting better and improving each night. In time and with patience I became increasingly better. My confidence improved, my presentation skills improved, my public-speaking skills improved, my sales improved, and in turn the money I made from sales improved. Going door to door was an amazing feeling. I learnt the value of building relationships. I realised the only reason someone buys from you is because of the relationship you form with them.

I encourage anyone that wants to get better in their life, their love life, in any aspect of being social, to learn to sell. You're always selling yourself, whether at an interview, on a date, or to a friend, neighbor or child. You're always giving and always receiving.

I continued selling for four years, from age twenty-four to twenty-eight. At that time I wasn't growing financially, my wealth wasn't increasing at all, but I was learning so much about the mind, human psychology, and how the world worked from mental, spiritual and financial points of view. All that I was learning came together in my mind until I realised that it wasn't just about making money. Success is about living a balanced life.

I stopped selling because I got the value that I needed and I was ready for the next step in my evolution.

INTRODUCED TO PROPERTY

At that time I was dancing with the idea of getting into property. I didn't know anything about it and I was introduced to an off-the-plan property in Balmain for half a million dollars, which required a $50,000 deposit.

I was very close to buying, very close to signing the contract. I knew nothing better to compare the deal with. Once again, a 'guardian angel' came to me. Funnily enough it was one of my clients from door-to-door selling.

She said, 'You know, I know this person that buys a lot of properties. Why don't you talk to him?'

'Why not?', I thought.

I met the guy and found out that he and his business partner had about 120 properties. *'Wow! That's a lot!'*, I thought to myself. *'This guy is onto something.'* That's the value of being open to meeting new people and being willing to learn from others.

So there I was with my borrowed $50,000 – ready to buy one property. Fortunately before I made that final decision I learnt quickly that you don't need to go and buy a half-million-dollar house. You can buy a cheaper house, put less money into in and then have more savings to buy into multiple investments.

The very first property I bought was a unit in West Sydney. I was what you call 'green'. I bought it without any real knowledge of whether it was a good deal or not and at that time I didn't understand the concept of renovating or adding value.

I bought it for $155,000 and rented it for $200 a week. Then the tenants left, leaving the property damaged. I went to the insurance company and secured a payout for the damages. From that I renovated my first property by default. For the renovations, I used a group of tradespeople who were painting for a friend of mine. To this day they're still the people I use. It's a very good relationship

That experience was a lesson in converting every challenge into an opportunity. Some people would freak out because of bad tenants. Some would say the tenants leaving was another problem, and then there was the damage they'd caused. **'Convert every challenge into an opportunity'** is now my motto. And that property is currently worth about $230,000.

Within three months of my first property going up in value as a result of the renovations, I organised the deposit and the money to purchase my second property. From then on I was basically buying a new property every three months.

Doing this was extremely exciting. When you buy property you technically buy money. You're getting a mortgage but you're also holding onto wealth. As opposed to working, property is something that is physically valuable, independent of yourself. Income follows assets. As long as you continue feeding your assets your income will follow.

DREAM, DESIGN, DO!

Two years after buying my first property, at the end of 2011, I had a portfolio of ten properties valued at $2,500,000 with equity of $700,000.

After appearing in several property investing magazines, people from everywhere began contacting me asking questions like **'How did you do it?', 'Where did you find the time?'** and **'Who did you learn from?'**

I answered all these questions and gave away plenty of advice for free. I realised I enjoyed that, and so I founded **Dream, Design, Do!** as the next step in my adventure.

With **Dream, Design, Do!** I guide and mentor clients from start to finish through their own property investment journeys. I work according to their needs, not only through education and mentoring, but actually by finding them properties they can buy as well as strategising why they want to invest.

That's what the rest of this book is about. It will take you through the journey that I take my clients on – so that you too can dream, design and do!

CHAPTER 2: WHY DO YOU WANT TO INVEST?

So that's my story – the steps I took and the journey I went on that got me where I am today.

I often say to myself that all the mistakes I've made are for other people's benefit. So I hope you've learnt and gathered lessons for yourself so far!

But before we continue I must ask you one very important question: **Why?**

Why are you reading this book?

That's the first thing I ask my clients when I meet them.

'Why what?!', they often exclaim.

'Why are you here?', I go on. **'Why did you come to see me?'**

I understand that this can be an awkward first question to ask. However, it's better to uncover the truth of a situation than progress on hazy assumptions.

Responses to the question are usually **'I read about you in Property Investing Australia. I want to have a portfolio of ten properties too'.** Or **'One of my friends saw you and said they got results. I want results as well'.**

Answers like these, though valid, don't really address the question.

When I ask 'Why?', I'm looking for the deep underlying reasons. I do not mean to be an annoying philosopher or existentialist. I ask

With strong powerful reasons you will go on to succeed, achieve all your goals, and more.

If you don't have a strong 'why' you will fail. You may experience initial wins but you'll soon run out of energy and motivation. This is why your 'why' is crucial. It's the fuel that keeps you going.

THE STUDENT WHO DID NOT KNOW WHY

I once had a student who was very keen to get started on his property investment journey. I asked him what his goal was. He replied, 'To have a portfolio of five properties'.

> I thought to myself. *'We can do this, no problem.'*

But when I asked him to dig deep and find his motivations and reasons he asked that we go straight into looking for a property and start purchasing and forget about examining his 'why'.

TOP TIP: *When you're paying someone to teach you, listen to what they have to say.*

To cut a long story short he failed in his goal. After buying his first property he decided to stop. He wanted to try out shares and see how he'd go there. I was disappointed to see him leave.

Unfortunately some students don't pay enough attention to the 'why', only spending a few cursory minutes on it. I have had clients who bought one or two properties and made a lot of money out of them. However, after that they lost motivation and put investing on the back burner, choosing instead to focus on something new, or on what they were doing before. Those clients didn't spend enough time opening up and learning, so they couldn't sustain the investing journey they started.

To succeed at property, to succeed in anything worth doing in life, you must be very clear on your reasons why. When unexpected difficulties arise and your commitment is tested, unless you are crystal clear on why you're doing what you're

The reverse also holds true. If you know why you're doing something, then you can meet any difficulty and continue.

AN ANALOGY: RUNNING YOUR RACE

Jim, Jill and Jack set a goal to run a marathon. They're excited! This is a big challenge and way out of all their comfort zones.

Jim is running the race to raise money for cancer research. His beloved brother died of cancer a month beforehand, so for him running the race is a way to remember and commemorate his brother. As the race progresses his knees and feet start to throb a little. That throbbing becomes a screaming pain and he's still got twelve kilometers to go …

Jill is running as she loves overcoming physical challenges. By climbing mountains, running endurance events and doing things she previously thought impossible she feels a rush of inner strength and confidence. When she overcomes challenges in her physical world she feels that she can meet any other challenge that comes her way. The pain begins, but it doesn't even matter …

Jack is running because he likes the free Powerade people get at the end. He thinks it'll be really cool to get free Powerade. Then the pain begins …

Who do you think will complete their goal? Who do you think will overcome the challenges that present themselves?

If you say 'Jack', I refuse to take you on as a client!

Both Jim and Jill will succeed at their goals. The challenges they face mean nothing in comparison to the payoff they'll get by finishing the race. Actually, the challenges deepen their resolve. After running this race they'll probably go on to run many more.

I use this analogy to highlight a few things. The first is that 'why' adopts different forms for different people. Secondly, your 'why' must have real emotional meaning for you. If it's superficial like

FINDING YOUR WHY

If I've done my job correctly you should now be convinced about the value of knowing your 'why'!

Before you answer 'why' it's helpful to know what your goal is. You're here because you're interested in property investing as a strategy to becoming wealthy I presume.

What specifically is your goal around property?

Write it down. Grab some paper, or your phone, tablet, laptop, or anything you can write with. Write 'My goal around property is to …' and then fill in your goal.

Some people's goals are to have a portfolio of four properties. Others are content with one. Some people think really big and say one hundred. All answers are OK. It's your goal, no one else's. So write a goal that's genuinely yours.

If your goal is something vague like **'I want a large profitable portfolio',** I want you to turn it into something solid that you can confidently say out loud.

It may help you to use the **SMART** method of stating your goal. **SMART** is the acronym for:

S – SPECIFIC

M – MEASURABLE

A – ACTIONABLE

R – RISKY

T – TIMEFRAME

An example of a **SMART** goal:

'My goal is to have a portfolio of fifty-seven properties by December 2016'.

'Fifty-seven properties' is a measurable result and 'by December 2016' is the timeframe in which to attain this result. It's these features that make the goal specific and actionable.

'R' is for risky. Some people say 'realistic' but what's the point in being realistic? Be unrealistic in your demands and expectations and you'll surprise yourself at what you can achieve. Even if you don't, a risky goal that scares and excites you in equal measure is a better goal to pursue, as you'll end up in a place higher than if you just went along with a 'realistic' goal.

Now for the most important part – **WHY?** Why is this your goal?

Please write down one hundred reasons.

YES – one hundred reasons. Grab a sheet of paper or open up a new document and get yourself comfortable. It'll take you a while.

Take your time with this. Expect it to take a lot of energy from you. You're examining the deepest truths in your subconscious and the answers won't come quickly.

Very often the first thirty reasons are the reasons you *believe* you have your goal. They're often what you think your reasons should be based on society's values and expectations that you've unconsciously taken on board. By the time you've written thirty reasons down the real reasons start to surface and you have clarity around your motivations and driving force.

HAVE YOU WRITTEN YOUR ONE HUNDRED REASONS YET?

You may notice in your one hundred reasons that a pattern will start to emerge. The same things will pop up again and again. These are your 'whys'. They're your friends now. They will propel you forward.

My 'why' is that I want to press the accelerator and see how hard I can go. I want to see how high I can fly. I want to do more and see what my limits ***'How hard can I thrash this thing?'*** That way, when challenges present themselves, they don't work to stop me, but rather encourage me to press myself further and harder.

Another of my 'whys' is to be able to do what I want, how I want, whenever I want. To have complete emotional and financial freedom – enjoying life on the inside and the outside with people that I respect and love.

Note that your 'why' can change over time. My 'why' when I was younger was simply to survive. I was at the lowest order of Maslow's hierarchy of needs. I just wanted to secure my food and rent for each week and my permanent residency so I could call Australia home.

Be aware that your underlying reason why is always more than just money. 'Money' might be the answer that immediately comes up, but more than anything it's what money can give you and do for you that is the real reason. For example, money can mean security and comfort, more time with loved ones, more time to pursue passion projects ...

Money is a unit of exchange. If there was nothing to exchange it for it would be pretty worthless. (Ask the man with a suitcase full of cash who is lost in the desert.) If money is the only reason that you're doing things then you're going to have a hard time succeeding financially.

BEYOND WHY

Once you're clear on your 'why' and you're ready to go there are a few mindsets that will greatly assist you. They are patience, resilience and perseverance.

Knowing your 'why' isn't a magic bullet that will solve everything for you. You still need to go ahead and do what you have to do. Patience, resilience and perseverance will be your greatest friends on your journey.

PATIENCE

Accept that you are embarking on a journey and that, with continued

the way. Don't be in a rush to move along. Enjoy and be happy now, where you're at. If you rush through life always waiting and wanting the next thing over the horizon you'll soon find yourself dead, not having enjoyed any minute of the process. As you take continual action, be patient and know that building something significant takes time end effort.

RESILIENCE

Resilience is being courageous within yourself. It means being tough enough to withstand challenges and not falter when things get tough. As the saying goes, 'When the going gets tough the tough get going'. The more you practice resilience the stronger it becomes. You can practice resilience by doing things that you find hard and that scare you. Surrounding yourself with resilient people helps too.

PERSISTENCE

Persistence is a function of both patience and resilience. To be persistent means you go on – you continue moving forward despite the difficulty. Knowing why helps here. If you don't know why you're doing something it's only a matter of time before you give up and move onto something shinier.

Nothing in the world can take the place of persistence. Talent will not; nothing is more common than unsuccessful individuals with talent. Genius will not; unrewarded genius is almost a proverb. Education will not; the world is full of educated derelicts. Persistence and determination alone are omnipotent.

– Ray Kroc, founder of McDonalds

With me it was fifteen years of being patient until I became an 'overnight success'. Fifteen years of being patient and resilient, of being open to learning from others, and fifteen years of taking continual action

DREAM, DESIGN, DO

CHAPTER 3:
STRATEGIES THAT IT'S BEST YOU DON'T USE

In order to acquire ten properties in two years I implemented a certain strategy.

But before I go into detail on what I did and how I did it, you should be aware that there are many alternative strategies out there. To say mine is the only one is nonsense.

Like anything else in life, there are many strategies that can be used in property investing, so long as you know the goal and end result you're aiming for. *(See why what we covered in Chapter 2 is so important?)* One of life's fundamental truths is that there can be many paths to the same destination.

Say for example your goal is to get a date. There are many different strategies you can undertake. You can go online, set up profiles on matchmaking sites, find people on <meetup.com> or register for speed dating. You can also go for offline strategies, such as hitting the club, getting friends to set you up, or even just approaching and saying 'Hi' to that attractive stranger on the bus.

The point I wish to make is that all of these strategies are geared towards the same goal and end result, and that's you going on a date. The path each one takes you down is different, but they all eventually take you to the same place.

So, going back to the world of property investing, this chapter is about those other paths, and why I chose not to take them.

OFF THE PLAN

The first strategy I want to talk about is purchasing property **off**

The first thing you need to recognise – whether you know it already or not – is that land appreciates in value and buildings depreciate in value. What this means is that over time land gains value, while buildings lose value.

An investor can claim depreciation on their tax filings, but what this actually means is the overall worth of their building is declining. The same happens when you buy a computer for your business; you can depreciate it over a number of years as a tax benefit, as that computer is losing value as better, faster and more cutting-edge computers come onto the market. The same thing happens to bricks and mortar. They can be depreciated because they're actually losing value.

A percentage of a building's value is based on the value of the land it sits on. Over time, the value of the land slowly creeps up, meaning more and more of the building's value becomes based on the land. This happens because systems and infrastructure such as electricity, plumbing, roofing and windows deteriorate even when well maintained, and features that were once considered cutting-edge become obsolete. Also, an assessment of the site can conclude that the land itself is 'underused'. (For example, a residential property in the middle of an area experiencing commercial growth would be considered underused, as it's not the best use of that land in that area.)

Once the value of the land reaches a certain percentage of the total property value, the whole site becomes a magnet for property developers looking to make the best use of that land.

So how does this work with off-the-plan properties?

Let's say a developer finds an area of land that can be converted into a large development project – a big block of buildings, a big block of apartments, or a big block of houses.

The developer then sends an application to council to get approval for the development. However, what happens is (if the development gets approval) the developer then needs money to

In most cases the developer doesn't have the money to go and build, for example, ten apartments, so he or she will go to the bank to obtain funding (called construction funding, or development funding).

To provide construction/development funding to the developer, the bank needs some measure of security. The lenders want to know if the developer is reputable. They want to know if they're trustworthy and if they have a record of successful developments. The bank also wants to know the number of presales.

SO WHAT IS A PRESALE?

To the developer, a presale is basically a guarantee to the bank that if the developer is building ten apartments, five of them (for example) have already been presold to buyers.

That's where the definition for off-the-plan properties comes in. Off-the-plan purchasing means purchasing a property – a house or apartment – that has not yet been built. It's called 'off the plan' because the decision to purchase is based purely on plans and drawings.

The way it works is that the developer gets most of the architectural engineering and planning down, then produces a brochure to show what the property will look like in one year's time, for example. They get a marketing team involved, and they market the development to the retail population.

One of the motivations a developer uses to promote the purchase of off-the-plan properties is that they can say, 'In one year, when this property is built, it will be worth this amount of money'. For example, let's say there's a three-bedroom house in development and the developer says it's going to be worth $750,000 in one year. They can promote it as such to retail purchasers, because it's brand new. A brand new property can't be depreciated, and you can get better tax benefits as opposed to an established property.

The second motivator is that the property can be negatively

maintain than the rental income it brings in. For example, a property may bring in $500 a week in rent, but actually cost you $1000 a week to maintain. This would leave you out of pocket $500 a week. A developer may use negative gearing as a way to promote a property, because as you (the property owner) are losing that money as an expense, you can claim it as a tax deduction and get tax credited to your return, so you pay less tax overall.

Those are the ways developers promote off-the-plan properties, and they're also the core benefits for investors. But here are the issues I have with them:

When you buy an off-the-plan property, you're basically paying full retail price. You may think, *'If I can get the property before it is even developed, then I'm making money from the beginning'. But* when you look at the end result, many people – architects, developers, the council, the original landowners – all have to make money from the project. And the money they make comes from your money. Factor that in and you'll realise you're paying full price.

So the reason I don't recommend off the plan is because you're paying the full value of a house when it might not be worth that much.

The second issue I have is: how do you know that a property will be worth what the developer *says* it will be worth in one year? You're speculating, right?

Because you don't know what's going to happen in one year. If the market is rising, yes, you'll make money, but that's not because you made money off the property – it's because the overall market went up. Once again, you're making a bet, you're gambling.

So what happens in some instances – especially if the market isn't particularly warm – is the property doesn't end up being valued at the price you agreed to buy it for, and you can't make the developer responsible because you signed a legal contract saying 'In one year I want to buy this property for this amount'. Fact is, the property doesn't get valued by the bank until it's built, and

For example, if you signed a contract with a developer to buy the property for $750,000 – but when it comes to ask the bank for funding and the market has dropped or the developer has over-speculated and the property is valued at only $650,000 – well, you still have to uphold the contract you signed for $750,000. Meaning you have to find the missing $100,000, and you often have to find it in cash. People can run into serious trouble when that happens. They can be forced to bounce the property off to someone else, often making a loss. That's just too risky in my view.

The other thing that people need to be aware of is that they simply don't know what the future holds. How do you know what's going to happen to you in that one-year period in terms of personal finances? What if you lose your job or are forced to change it? What if you have to go overseas? What if your partner can't work anymore? If your financial circumstances change during the building process you might not be able to get a loan for $750,000 anymore, even if the property is valued at $750,000. The bank may not want to lend you *anything* based on your new circumstances.

That's why I stay away from buying off the plan.

BRAND NEW HOMES

The next strategy I want to mention is that of buying brand new homes. The reason I tell clients to avoid buying new homes as property investments is that you can't really tell how much your property is worth. When considering a brand new property, you must ask yourself if it's worth the price you're paying. A correct price for a brand new property is hard to determine because it hasn't been given sufficient time in the market to establish itself.

Buying a brand new home is a bit like buying a brand new car. Consider buying a brand new Toyota. The price you pay for a brand new Toyota is markedly different when compared to the price of a model that's exactly the same but five years old. True – a brand new property is not exactly like buying a brand new car as we know that, over time, the property will grow in value. But there still is a high chance of overpaying. And that's the point I want to push across. As an investor, you run the risk of paying money you shouldn't have to.

I recommend investors stick to buying properties at least five years old. That way the market has had enough time to test the property's value. Anything less than five years old simply hasn't had enough time to establish an accurate price.

PICKING THE NEXT SHORT-TERM HOT SPOT

The first thing I want to mention about buying property in so-called hot spots is that there are short-term hot spots and long-term hot spots. I have nothing against buying in long-term hot spots; in fact, I encourage it. But I want to talk about short-term hot spots here and why I don't recommend buying into them.

So what exactly is a short-term hot spot?

The best example I can provide is that of the mining areas. People think, *'I'll go and invest in this area because mining is about to boom'*, and just pick a location because there's going to be a new mine nearby.

In Australia, that's likely to be in the middle of nowhere, with very little supporting infrastructure. So the first problem is, if the property is just land without a building, it will likely cost a whole lot extra to have anything developed on it.

Sure, there's money to be made if you know how to get in at the right time, but you also have to know the right time to get out. Because with every boom there's got to be a bust.

So the first issue I have with picking areas relating to the mining boom is what happens if the mine suddenly has to close? Because your property is in the middle of nowhere, who is going to want it after that? And what happens to the properties themselves after a sudden drop in value?

To capitalise on short-term hot spots, you need to know when

But 'getting out' brings to me the second issue. Even if you do know when to get out, and sell to somebody else, you give that buyer a shred of doubt. He's thinking, *'Is this the next hot spot, or am I going to lose money here?'*, when in fact just by selling you're pretty certain he will lose money. In a way, you're doing that person over. Even if you do make your profit, you still invoke bad karma. I believe in karma – 'what goes around comes around' – and selling to somebody under such circumstances just brings about bad karma. It'll bite you back later on down the road.

So I don't believe in investing in short-term hot spots. What I believe investors should be doing instead is picking the next long-term hot spot.

What I do to pick out long-term hot spots is look at the potential longevity of growth in an area. I ask, *'In fifteen years, is this area going to continue to boom? Is it going to experience continuous growth in population, infrastructure, migration, schooling and so on?'* These are all things I look for when assessing the long-term prospects of an area.

So how can you identify these long-term hot spots?

Basically, I recommend that you look at council approvals from developers. Find out what big developments are happening in what areas. I recommend this because most big developers do their own research, and do it well.

Another tip is to see which areas have the most big corporations going in – for example, McDonalds, Bunnings, Coles. Corporations like these often have huge research teams, and if they're opening somewhere it means they've done the market research to best determine where to continue their growth. Chains like these often follow infrastructure development – where money is being spent on transport, train lines, roads, schooling, education and so on. It pays to look into where this kind of funding is going because these are the next long-term hot spots.

PROPERTIES OVER $500K

Investing in properties valued at half a million or more is another strategy, but I don't use it. If you start purchasing high-value properties, for example a million-dollar property, you need a minimum $200,000 to get into that property. So let's say you come to me with $200,000 in savings – at maximum you might be able to get into one or two properties.

However, let's imagine you do buy that million-dollar house. So now you hold a million dollars worth of property, with all your savings in one location, probably an affluent, high socioeconomic area. What I'm getting at is, 'Don't put all your eggs in one basket'.

What you need to be aware of is that all banks have the right to ask you to invest more cash into your loan if your security property price drops and so your **loan-to-value ratio (LVR)** becomes unacceptably high to them. Banks can also change the LVR % they are willing to offer you over time (more detail on the loan-to-value ratio is on page 58).

In a worst case scenario like a global financial crisis, that $1,000,000 house that you bought with an $800,000 loan (80% LVR initially) crashes down to a $500,000 valuation. This LVR is lower than the initial 80% LVR they accepted, as they may be implementing a more conservative lending policy after the GFC. So your bank will now only lend you 70% LVR x $500,000 = $350,000 total.

However you still owe them the full $800,000 loan they initially extended to you. This means you must pay them $450,000 cash to reduce your total borrowings from $800,000 to $350,000. Very few people have $450,000 cash available to them, especially in a liquid form that they can access quickly to pay down their bank loan. So what happens in that scenario? The bank repossesses and takes control of your security property in order to sell it to recover as much as possible of the $800,000 loan that it initially extended to you. This is a situation referred to as 'mortgagee in posession'.

Where does that leave you? You have lost all your $200,000 savings

against you. Clearly, this is a big setback that will take significant time to recover in your investment journey.

While you cannot escape this risk altogether, you can manage and minimise this risk by using your $200,000 savings, for the sake of this example, to invest into multiple properties of much lower price, under $500,000 each. The total value of all those properties may well exceed $1,000,000, but you only have a small risk/exposure in any one property.

This is a simple illustration of the value of diversifying your portfolio. Diversification is a well recognised investment principle, and you need to remember that it applies to investing in property, in just the same way that it applies to any other asset class.

CASE STUDY

I've had numerous clients who have attempted the above strategies during their property investment journeys, and all ended up getting burnt. And by burnt I mean forced into a period of financial hardship. Truth is, the majority of my clients can be burnt. Here are some examples of how, and how badly.

I had one client who did indeed purchase off the plan at $750,000. He gave the deposit to the developer, and the developer said the property would be worth $750,000 in one year. However, after that year had rolled by and it came time to buy, the property was only valued by the bank at $650,000. The client was then forced to resell the property to keep the developer off their back, and they're still paying the remaining $100,000. They got burnt quite badly.

I had another client who decided to invest in a brand new home, and bought it for $750,000 again. But after five years, the property was still worth $750,000. The problem here is they paid far too much initially. They really should have paid $600,000. So they haven't made any money with that property and all their savings

TROUBLESHOOTING

The best advice I can give regarding the strategies in this chapter is not to implement them in the first place!

But of course that isn't the best advice for those already getting burnt.

For people who have already made an investment based on these strategies – particularly off-the-plan purchasing – the best advice I can offer is simply to be patient. If you've made a loss, you have to be patient and wait until your property goes up in value. Eventually it will. Or, if you believe that you should sell, then sell. Make a loss and walk away.

Regardless of whether you lose money, or even gain money after you lose money, you need to treat your experience as a lesson. A lesson in getting out and living on. Because regardless of what hardships you encounter, you can always endure them. In some cases you're going to have to. Eventually make you'll make your way out the other side.

Many clients have come to me while they're in the process of getting burnt, and this is one of the first things I tell them. Patience is a vital mindset to adopt, not just when suffering the stress of a bad financial investment, but for any sort of hardship life delivers. Just remind yourself to be patient. Nothing lasts forever, and life will go on.

For people who haven't made a bad investment yet, I recommend they think twice about what advice they take from other people, particularly when it comes to the strategies outlined in this chapter, as sometimes that advice may not be in your best interests. People have all sorts of agendas and plans of their own.

If you're going to work with someone on this, you need to make sure you're always working towards your own goals, and not somebody else's.

CHAPTER 4:
THE STRATEGY I USED TO BUY 10 PROPERTIES IN 2 YEARS

Now that we've covered a whole heap of strategies I didn't use, let's talk about the strategies I did use – the strategies that allowed me to buy on average a new investment property every three months.

I'm going to share with you all the knowledge behind these strategies, and be as transparent as possible, so that you too can follow the same steps and achieve financial success for yourself.

BUYING IN ESTABLISHED SUBURBS

The first strategy I used was buying into established suburbs.

An established suburb is an area that has a history of factual financial data. It has schools, transport infrastructure, houses, apartments, and a community of people that have been there for more than fifty years. But why buy into it?

For one simple, important reason: there is historical data to track.

As mentioned, investing in property involves taking risks. But by analysing historical data we can make those risks calculated ones. You can see what trends are taking place or have taken place, as opposed to investing in a brand new area where there is no data to provide you with information. It's practically guesswork in such scenarios.

Investing in established suburbs also involves guesswork, but in some sense you can 'predict' the future because you can base

data you can sift through. You can find out what market prices have been like over fifty years. What growth has been like. What rental yields have been like. What type of people rent in the suburb, how many have mortgages and how many are owner-occupiers. All of this data tells you the demographics of the suburb. By knowing those demographics and how they've grown and changed you'll be better able to predict trends.

You'll also have increased insight into the suburb and be better informed on whether you're getting a good deal. For example, if you buy a property for $200,000 but the market comparables in the area are $250,000, you'll know you've found a good investment.

You won't be able to do that in a brand new development. All you have to go on there is what the developer tells you. For example, you might get told, 'This is worth $500K, but I'm giving it to you for $400'. Well how do you really know it's worth 500? It's a brand new property, and thus has no established price. You need to have market forces present to establish a price.

Now that you know the importance of data tracking, where do you get that data from?

I recommend the website <rpdata.com.au>. It has all the data any Australian investor could want.

WHAT TO LOOK FOR

Once you've got all the data you need about the particular suburb you're looking at investing into, you need to know what specific data points to look at.

The first points you should look at are **median house prices**, **median unit prices**, and **capital growth** in the area. You'll want to find out whether there has been growth, or if there has been a decline.

The next points to look at are **rental demand** and **rental yield**. How many people are renting? What is the percentage of owner-

determine whether it's a highly rentable area. If it is then the rental yields would appear to be going up in the data.

Another important data point to investigate is what the **mortgage finance** is like in the area. This will tell you how many people own their own homes and how many still have debt on their homes. This is important because it tells you how wealthy the suburb is. If more people have paid off their home loans then the population you're investing into is generally more affluent.

Simply speaking, you can judge how wealthy an area is by how many people have paid off their mortgage. A good thing to see when analysing this data point is a medium balance between renters and homeowners. The reason I look for the number of people renting is because that signifies an increased rental demand. The more people that rent in an area, the more demand there is, which means I can push up my rental prices.

You should also look for **income** and **occupation**. What types of jobs do people in the area have? What is the average income?

These points give you a valuable understanding of the area. The important thing to look for here is how many people are working and how many are unemployed. If there is a high percentage of unemployment, then you'll know it's not exactly one of the best areas. If you invest in such an area, be aware that rent may not be so easy to get. That said, it doesn't matter if it's a low-income area as long as there is some sort of paid employment. Paid employment means tenants that are able to pay their rent.

BUYING UNDER MARKET VALUE

The second strategy I stuck by was buying under market value.

The key to buying under market values is defining market value in the first place. So what is market value?

Simply put, **market value** is what you pay for something. What's the market value for an apple? What's the market value for a

When you're looking at a house and want to define its market value, you can compare it with other houses with similar characteristics. This is comparing apples with apples.

There are so many characteristics to a property: two bedroom, three bedroom, one bedroom, four bedroom with a duplex, one bathroom, two bathroom, and so on and on.

So what I mean when I say 'apples with apples' is, if you're looking to purchase a three-bedroom house on a 600 square metre block, then you want to compare it to other three-bedroom houses on 600 square metre blocks. Don't compare it to a four bedroom, or a three-bedroom apartment, because those are entirely different characteristics. You're not comparing apples with apples anymore – you're comparing an apple to an orange and a mango.

To accurately define a property's market value, find ten other 'apples' and work out the average price among them. So for example if your 'apple' is indeed a three-bedroom house on a 600 square metre block, then find ten other three-bedroom houses on 600 square metre blocks. The average price of those ten properties is then your definition of market value.

So what is buying under market value?

When you work out the average of your ten three-bedroom, 600 square metre block houses (let's say $550,000), buying under market value would be buying a three-bedroom 600 square metre block house at anything lower than $550,000.

Now there is a specific reason I mention buying under market value as an actual investment strategy, as this is more than just a 'discount' or a 'saving'.

By buying under market value you are actually making money on the way in. Following the above example, if you buy your three-bedroom, 600 square metre block house for $500,000 when the average market value is $550,000, then you make $50,000 as soon as you sign the dotted line.

You might hear a lot of investors talk with pride about their capital growth. However, it's most likely that's the only thing they have. They paid market value or even overpaid for their property when they bought it and now have to wait for growth in the economy over time to increase its value.

But by buying under market value you can make money from the get go and rely on capital growth second. This way you enter the game winning.

NEGOTIATING

Your question now might be, *'How do I go about buying under market value?'*

Here is one way – negotiation.

Negotiation is simply working to get the best deal happening.

If you go to get your car washed in an established, standard car wash it can cost you $40 in a good area. But did you know if you go on a rainy day you can get the same service for $25? Did you also know that if you say 'It's a rainy day, I'd like to pay $25' then the car washers would likely say 'Yes'?

The reason is supply and demand. The car wash is always paying for a supply of workers, and on a rainy day there's no demand for their services. Who gets their car washed when it's raining?

So how do you go about successfully negotiating a deal on the property market?

The number one tip is **just ask**. Simply put, if you don't ask you don't get. If you rock up to that car wash on a rainy day and don't ask if you could pay $25, you'll pay $40 instead, guaranteed.

The very same goes for investing in property. If there's a property you're looking at buying that's on the market for X dollars but you'd like to buy it for less, just ask if you can buy it for less.

Asking for what you want has a power that carries over into all areas of life. For example, if there's someone that catches your eye, the easiest way to get them to go on a date with you is to just ask. Never underestimate the power of asking – it's the easiest way to get what you want!

It's also happens to be the simplest way to identify if it's a rainy day in the property market.

My number two tip is properly **guiding the negotiation** to where you want it to go.

You need to develop an artistic, tactical way of negotiating. There is finesse to it. Always start with the end goal in mind. Don't reveal what your end goal is, but rather influence the other person in a way that eventually leads to it.

Say for example you're interested in a property you know to be worth $300,000 and you've decided the maximum you want to pay is $290,000. Do you really say you are going to pay $290,000?

No, of course not.

Instead you offer $250,000. When you deliver your $250,000 offer the agent by law needs to take it to the seller or vendor. The agent might be saying to themselves, 'That is ridiculous', but they're legally responsible for relaying the offer. That itself gives you an opportunity to win. It puts the owner under pressure to consider, *'Maybe I could do this for 250?'* And I have won many deals just by doing that. It's one way of winning.

The second way of winning is if the owner comes back asking for 295. You respond by saying 270, to which he says 290. And there you are – right at the goal you originally set before commencing the negotiation. You have now won because you're paying $10,000 less than the established market value of $300,000. You've effectively made $10,000.

From there you could push it even further by offering 289 instead,

you in a serious winning position as you were committed to only paying $10,000 less but you managed even less than that again.

That's a basic walkthrough of negotiation. The last thing that needs to be mentioned about it is the position, or **mindset**, you're coming from when you enter the negotiation. It's probably the most important aspect.

To let you in on what I do, I always place deliberate emphasis and importance on the fact that I'm the only person interested and there is no one else. Logically I know the world is buying, but in my eyes it's raining and no one is buying.

When you come into a negotiation from such a position, you'll be far more likely to end up successful. Remember, it's about asking for what you want, and asking with confidence. The same can be applied to everything else in life!

BUYING RUN-DOWN PROPERTIES

The third way of bringing down market value is by buying properties that are not always in the best condition. When the building report comes in and reads 'This is broken, that needs to be fixed, etc.' I can go back to the agent or owner and say 'This is going to cost me X dollars to fix. You need to reduce the price'.

Say for example you have your eye on a run-down house valued on the market at $300,000. The builder does his report and estimates it will cost $50,000 to repair all the damage. Do you go to the owner and ask for $50,000 less than market value?

No.

You ask for $80,000 less. Because you're the person who has to pay the cost of repairing the building and you have to value that. And you know that anyone else buying the property has to pay that too. Most people don't want a property if there's a problem, so demand drops. And when there's no demand, the price comes down. This is how you can get a 'rainy day' on the property market.

FORCING VALUE

Another strategy I used was forcing value.

Forcing value is the domain of renovations. It's the reason you renovate a property, or purchase a run-down property you can improve.

Often what happens is you can bump up a property's market value through renovating, thereby increasing the value of your portfolio. It's worth getting a building report commissioned into any building you feel needs or would benefit from a renovation. If the cost of the proposed renovations is less than the difference between the amount you bought or will buy the property for and the estimated value of the property once renovations are complete, then go ahead and renovate!

Think of forcing value as another way of making money on the way in. For example, if it costs $5000 to do a renovation that will add $25,000 to the property's market value, that's $20,000 you'll make right there. You don't have to rely on capital growth for the value of the property to rise – you can make it rise yourself! Hence why it's called 'forcing value'.

Renovations are a complex topic however, and the concept of forcing value simply states *why* you should do them. Details on to do them are covered extensively in a later chapter.

AN OVERALL NEUTRAL PORTFOLIO

The last strategy I used on my path to property success was developing and maintaining an overall neutral portfolio.

When you invest in property there is a concept called 'gearing'. Gearing comes in three varieties: negative, positive and neutral.

Negative gearing basically means that a property costs you more money than it makes for you. Then there is **positive gearing**, which means that a property makes you more money than it costs

income you receive from your property is equivalent to the money going out to maintain it.

For a first investment, I recommend purchasing a neutrally geared property. The property should have mortgage repayments going out that are equal to the rental payments coming in. The reason for this is that it has no effect on borrowing capability, making it much easier for an investor to borrow money to fund their next purchase.

The concept of gearing can also be applied to collective portfolios as well as individual properties.

I believe that your overall portfolio needs to stay neutral. And by overall portfolio I mean all your individual properties put together.

The reason I say it needs to stay neutral is because there is nothing wrong with having a negatively geared property – they are in fact great for attaining capital growth. As long as the next property you purchase is positively geared. So if one property is costing you $200 a week, you want your next property to make you $200 a week. That way your property portfolio is self-sufficient.

There are two important reasons for having a self-sufficient portfolio.

Number one is that your job or business is not dependent upon it. If you ever lose your business, business income or job, then your property is not at risk. It's self-sustaining – looking after itself in terms of income and expenditure.

The second reason is that if you're building a portfolio you need to keep going back to the bank to borrow more money.

CASE STUDY

A property I was looking at purchasing was a bit run down. I asked for a building report on the approximate cost of renovations. The report estimated the renovations would cost $10,000.

DREAM, DESIGN, DO

I set it as my goal to purchase the property for $200,000. In order to get there, I offered $180,000. After a bit of back and forth, I did indeed purchase the property for the $200,000 target I had set.

Now that I owned the property, I carried out the renovations I had in mind, for the set price of $10,000. They were completed in four weeks, and raised the value of the property substantially. It's now valued on the market at $250,000. So basically in four weeks I made $40,000.

CHAPTER 5: FINANCE

Finance is the nitty-gritty of the investing journey. You don't have to be a book-cooking wizard, but you do have to have a solid understanding of the basics.

GEARING

We've already mentioned gearing several times, but now is the time to discuss it in depth.

Gearing is a label given to a property to determine its state of cash flow. Gearing comes in three varieties: negative, positive and neutral.

Negative gearing means that the cash flow coming in from a property – for example rental income – is less than the expenses or outgoings. To make it even simpler: the property is costing you money.

The first and most important expense is the property's mortgage or loan repayments. Many people judge gearing by looking at rental income and comparing it to mortgage payments. If the loan repayment exceeds the rent then gearing is negative. If the rental income exceeds the loan repayment then it's positive. I consider this a flawed approach.

There are many different expenses to factor into negative gearing. When I look at negative gearing I look at it from two different points – gross and net.

Gross negative gearing is where you're just looking at the property's loan repayment against its rental income. **Net negative gearing** on the other hand is factoring in all associated costs of the property. The first and most important expense is always the property's mortgage or loan repayments. But there are also water rates, council rates, landlord insurance, building insurance,

apartment block, and maintenance issues. Bottom line is, if it's going to cost me money, I add it into the cost. It's from there that I determine whether a property is negative, neutral or positively geared.

Something I should call extra attention to are property management fees. They are a fee you pay to have someone else manage your property – as opposed to managing the tenant and property yourself. By hiring a property manager you never have to deal with anything directly. A property manager will collect rent for you, ensure everything is in order and keep the garden tidy, amongst everything else. I strongly recommend having a property manager to manage your properties, as your expertise is investing and their expertise is managing tenants. Think of it as an outsourced job (and see Chapter 8 for a further discussion about why an outsourcing mindset is useful).

Normally what happens in Australian real estate is that the closer your property is to the centre of any large city, such as Sydney, Melbourne or Adelaide, the higher the negative gearing. The more distant from a city centre a property is, the higher the rental yields.

RENTAL YIELDS

Rental yield is calculated by dividing the total amount of rent collected for a year by the purchase price of your property.

When I look for properties for myself or my clients, I only look for properties with a rental yield of 6% or higher. That means the property is overall (including council rates, water and so on) going to be neutral or slightly positively geared.

HOW GEARING CAN GROW OR STALL YOUR PORTFOLIO

Now, the thing is when it comes city proximity, rents are lower but capital growth is higher. Generally speaking, properties close to inner cities will grow in value faster than properties in suburbs and regional areas. This is great to know, and the core benefit of negatively geared properties, that means your job or business income has to support your property portfolio.

If you happen to have a property that's slightly negatively geared that's OK. By 'slightly negatively geared' I mean the property costs you no more than $400 a month. Four hundred dollars a month is OK on an income of $100,000 a year but definitely no less than that. And if you're earning less than that then the property purchases you make should be even less negatively geared.

The reason for this is because if you want to apply for a loan to finance another property, you'll have to prove to the bank you can support the second purchase.

For example, let's say you bought a property close to the city and it was costing you $400 a month to maintain, and you wanted to buy an identical property. That property is also going to cost you $400 a month, meaning your total outgoings are $800 a month. You'd have to save $800 from your income every month to maintain your properties.

What can happen now is the bank might decline your application for that or a future property purchase. Hence you've stalled yourself from continuing to invest in property. Your journey stops there.

REAPING CAPITAL GROWTH

So how does one grow a portfolio beyond one or two investments?

Let's say you've stalled your portfolio with only one investment purchase, a $400,000 asset in Sydney. In Sydney, property on average appreciates at 7% per year. So in terms of capital gain, your net worth is only going up $28,000 a year.

But if you kept your portfolio neutral or positive and were able to continue to borrow money for multiple properties that were either neutral or positive, your gearing can be spread across the entire portfolio. Then you can grow your asset base.

For example, in my case I now have an asset base of over $3,000,000 that increases in worth by roughly $25,000 a month – but the only reason I was able to acquire that asset base is because I was allowed to borrow money from the banks when those properties weren't costing me any money to maintain.

WHICH LENDER TO USE

Now that we're on the topic of borrowing money, it's time to talk about which lender to use.

There are many different types of banks. There are what I call the first-tier banks, which are the 'big four' – the Commonwealth Bank, ANZ, NAB and Westpac. Then there are the second-tier banks, for example St. George, BankWest and Suncorp. Then you have the third-tier banks, which are your small lenders like Liberty Financial.

All these banks have different criteria for how they lend money.

And regardless of which bank you end up borrowing from, you need to keep the bank as your best friend.

As long as you don't have the cash to go buy a property yourself, you want to treat the bank like your friend and partner, and not someone who sucks your money. The only reason you're able to invest in property at all is because there's a bank out there that has money and is willing to lend it to you. If that bank didn't exist, you wouldn't be able to get the money from anyone else, with the exception of that dodgy guy out the back of the casino who charges 90% interest and accepts payments of limbs as well as cash.

There's a strategy to choosing a lender, just like there's a strategy to choosing a property. To me it's about choosing the bank that allows you to borrow the easiest amount of money according to the fewest criteria. What I mean by that is, which bank is willing to (for example) give you a $250,000 loan while asking the minimal number of questions?

THE WAY BANKS WORK

Let's say you're looking at taking out that $250,000 loan with two different banks – **Bank A** or **Bank B**.

Bank A charges an interest rate of 7% and Bank B charges an interest rate of 5%. That 2% can make a big difference to what you'll be paying back monthly, and this links back to gearing. The bank and loan you choose can determine whether your property is positively or negatively geared.

The bank charging 7% is likely to have fewer criteria for getting a loan because they know you're paying a higher premium. They cover their risks, even with asking fewer credit questions, because they know they'll be making money off you month by month. However, a bank that charges interest at 5% also knows they'll need to ask more questions to secure their loan – they'll naturally want to know about who you are and what you do with your money.

Then there are bank fees. With banks it's often a balancing act between interest rates and fees. Banks charge different interest rates, but they always make money one way or another from the loans you take out with them.

What I've noticed is, banks that charge higher interest rates often have lower fees, and when I talk about fees I mean all types – application fees, monthly fees, direct debit fees, admin fees, and on and on. There are many other fees in the fine print too. Banks that charge lower interest rates normally charge higher fees. Remember, banks will make their money one way or another.

MAKING THE CHOICE

Choosing a lender is strategic, and it's again about doing your research. I look at which bank is easiest to borrow money from, with good interest rates, minimum fees and a fast turnaround so they can process your application quicker.

on what questions they ask and whether that bank is right for the purchase I'm making (or my client is making).

DEPOSITS

Now that you've found the right lender you need to make a deposit. A deposit is the amount of money you have to put towards the property that the bank is going to secure. The deposit you'll need to put down is determined by the bank's current **loan-to-value ratio (LVR)**, which is a percentage indicating how much the bank will lend in comparison to how much the property you're buying is worth.

Back in the good days of financing, before the October 2008 global financial crisis, bank LVR, could be up to 100%, meaning you were able to borrow up to 100% of the property's value. You could buy a $250,000 property with no money or savings, as the bank would lend you $250,000 for it.

After the 2008 global financial crisis, LVRs dropped to around 80%, meaning you had to make a deposit of 20% in order to get a loan. That same $250,000 property would require you $50,000 in savings as deposit for it.

Banks lowered LVRs as a security measure, to stop people defaulting on their loans. The global financial crisis really hit overseas harder than Australia, but the banks here still decided to play it safe. Should a person here default on a $250,000 loan with an LVR of 80%, the bank would sell the property quickly on the market as a repossession, and be prepared to lose 20% of the property's value. By selling at 80% of the property's value, the bank would make back all the money the defaulter owed.

Right now (2013) LVRs are much better, sitting at about 95%. Hence the $250,000 property that once required a $50,000 deposit now requires only $12,500 down.

That's not to say LVRs might drop back to 80% (or even lower). They are simply where they are now because the economy has

Let's say you have $100,000 and are looking to invest in some $250,000 properties. In one scenario the LVR is 80%, and in the other it's 95%.

With the LVR at 80% you'll need to make $50,000 deposits, allowing you to invest in two properties. With the LVR at 95% a $250,000 loan will require only a $12,500 deposit, allowing you to invest in eight properties. So now you have an asset portfolio of $2,000,000 as opposed to $500,000.

INTEREST RATES

So this brings us to the topic of interest rates.

Interest rates are basically the cost of money. They are the percentage a borrower has to pay a lender for the privilege of using their money, whether it's an institutional lender, private lender or bank. Interest payments are calculated based on the amount of money borrowed and the term over which it (and the interest it generates) must be repaid – repayments can be weekly, fortnightly or monthly.

HOW INTEREST RATES ARE DETERMINED

Every country has a Reserve Bank – a central or governing bank – that oversees the monetary position of its country's economy and how that economy performs from day to day. For example, Australia's economy is monitored by The Reserve Bank of Australia.

The Reserve Bank meets monthly to review current and past economic figures and then makes forecasts based on its review. That's how it determines what interest rate to set; banks then follow on from that decision.

Now here's the thing; just because the Reserve sets an interest rate of, for example, 5%, does not mean that banks will charge you 5% on your loan. That is because 5% is actually what it costs the bank to borrow money from the Reserve. If banks borrow money from the Reserve at 5%, and then lend to you at 5%, they make zero

example it is 0.5% and the Reserve Bank's interest rate is 5.0%, the bank's interest rate will be 5.5%.

But how does the Reserve Bank determine the interest rate in the first place?

INFLATION

When determining the base interest rate, one of the first things the Reserve Bank looks at is inflation.

The most basic definition of **inflation** is how expensive things are going to be over a period of time.

Let's just say inflation is rising – and we have what is known as a 'rising market'. What that means is that prices are going up continuously – faster than the cost of living or the standard of living. That in turns means that the value of money is going down. For example, that one dollar you spent on a chocolate bar today could have bought two or three bars ten years ago, but might not be enough to buy even half a bar ten years from now. Put another way, thanks to inflation, that one dollar today was 'worth' more (bought more) in the past and will be worth less in the future (will buy less). That's how inflation works.

Another view of inflation is that when there is high supply of products or services and low demand for them, then prices are low or will fall. Conversely, if there is high demand and low supply, prices will rise. And when prices rise, the cost of things becomes more expensive (our definition of inflation) and thus inflation is on the rise.

In order to help control inflation and the economy the Reserve Bank monitors and alters the base interest rate (the cost of money). When interest rates rise, the cost of borrowing money goes up.

Business lending rates also go up. For example, a café owner who's just secured a $250,000 loan for his café now has to pay more money to the bank, and so the cost of running his business

At the same time, personal spending goes up because it costs us more money to buy food and coffee, as well as all sorts of other products and services – and this factor curbs or controls our spending.

For example, your home mortgage interest rate has just gone up. Your car loan repayment has just gone up. Your credit card repayment has just gone up, and all that flows through the economy.

When people start to reduce their spending then demand goes down, supply goes up, prices go down and thus inflation goes down. And that's how interest rates are controlled.

The other thing to note is that just because the Reserve Bank increases or reduces the interest rate, it doesn't mean that banks follow suit. If for example the Reserve Bank drops the interest rate by 0.25 points, banks aren't compelled to follow by 0.25 points. There's no legislation to force them to do so, and banks often have other factors and costs to consider. They can't just say, *'Well the Reserve Bank dropped it so we're going drop it by the same amount'*. They might drop it by 0.20 instead.

FIXED OR VARIABLE?

If you understand the basics of interest rates and how they're determined, you may also be familiar (especially as a homeowner or property investor) with the terms **fixed** and **variable**. These are the two main types of interest rates banks offer on their home loan packages.

Fixed

A **fixed interest rate** is a rate that doesn't change over a certain amount of time. For example, a bank might offer a fixed interest rate of 5% over five years. This means that for the first five years of paying off your home loan, the interest rate you're paying is 5% – regardless of whether the Reserve Bank pushes interest rates up or down after their monthly review. You can fix a rate for one year,

The main benefit of a fixed interest rate is that you can adequately forecast your repayments. As your repayments will be fixed for a certain amount of time you can properly plan and budget for future investments. You also have the security of knowing that if interest rates go up, yours will not. The downside is if interest rates do down, yours won't. Fixed interest rates are for those who seek greater certainty about how much they have to put towards things, or towards their property expenses.

A fixed interest rate is good to lock in when you know interest rates are at a low. You can never predict when they'll be at their lowest because that's everybody's dream, but you can go on what *fairly* low compared to the last few years. I would define anything around 5.5% to be low.

If you can fix a rate around the 5.5% mark it's a good sign. Banks are very good at forecasting the future of the economy; it's why they hire all those economists. If the banks are dropping their fixed interest rates on three-year loans that means they're aware (or at least they think) that the economy is going to be low. Likewise, if the banks are raising their fixed interest rates for three-year loans, that probably means the economy is going to start heating and hence that's why interest rates are going to go up.

The thing to be cautious about with fixed interest rates is that if you fix an interest rate and you want to move that loan from one bank to another, you're up for heavy penalties called **break costs**. Break costs are a fee the bank hits you with when you break a loan, because you cost the bank money. Fixed interest rates not only provide secure financial projections for you – the investor – but also for the bank. If you sign onto a fixed loan for three years, that's three years of profit the bank can safely rely on. By leaving the bank for another, you alter the first bank's financial position and a property that's an asset for them is no longer there. Break costs are a disincentive for making the switch.

The reason to switch home loans is straightforward and goes back to the earlier topic of which lender to choose. Banks change day to day, year to year, and if you believe there's a better lender out

Variable

A variable loan is easy to define. As the Reserve Bank goes along and changes its interest rate every month, a **variable interest rate** home loan will change along with it. Such loans don't give you the certainty a fixed rate does, but if interest rates are going down you'll be in an advantageous position as your repayments will be less. That said, if they go up you'll find yourself paying more.

WHICH ONE TO PICK

In a nutshell, it all depends on the state of the economy. If interest rates are low, choose fixed. If interest rates are high, take variable.

And if you're in any doubt, go to someone who has the knowledge and resources to give you an informed opinion that fits your investing strategy.

HANDLING LENDERS

As your portfolio grows, and you have multiple properties all with loans taken out on them, you'll inevitably come across the option of spreading your portfolio between multiple lenders as opposed to taking out all your loans with the same bank or institution. There are reasons for doing both.

If you're with a good bank that fits your criteria in terms of borrowing funds, ease of borrowing and interest rates, and you have an existing relationship with that bank, I highly recommend taking out your next property with them. They know who you are, and because you already have a relationship with them, there'll be less paperwork and fewer questions to answer. It's a bit like dating – if they're a good bank and you're happy with them, you'd be wise not to stuff them around and say you're going off to another bank for another loan. You instead want to build a relationship and, just like a potential partner, a bank is going to take you and your applications more seriously if you've shown them you're in it for the long term. When you go for your second, third, fourth (and more!) property, they'll look at you with much greater ease than if

That said, there comes a time when I advise my clients to move banks. The reason I would spread a portfolio between different lenders is that, in my opinion, the moment you have more than a million dollars worth of borrowings with one bank, you're considered a high risk.

Let's say there's a severe downturn in the economy, property values start to drop, and you have $2,000,000 worth of property with one bank. You will be on their radar because they know now that your $2,000,000 portfolio has gone down 50%. They know they're holding assets that are two million in bulk but actually only worth a million. So they have the ability to come to you and say you need to immediately pay down a million dollars worth of debt, for which you need to have a million dollars in cash. And if you don't they are in the position to say, **'Well we need to sell these properties and recoup the losses'.**

Now let's say you only have about $700,000 in borrowings with that bank. Of course, you're now not as risky as you were with two million. That's the reason why I would spread a portfolio through different banks, so that the risk is less to both parties. In uncertain conditions it's playing it safe. It doesn't mean it's a foolproof strategy, but you're buying time should the worst-case scenario happen, when property starts devaluing immediately.

Indeed, should the worst-case scenario happen, or if you were unable to make your monthly repayments, if you have your portfolio spread through multiple banks it's only one bank coming after you. The properties you have with other banks will be protected – provided of course you make those repayments.

For example, let's say you've lost your job and you need two months to get back on track. If you had all your loans with one bank and you weren't able to make one repayment, everything else is affected because your entire lending is with that bank.

In short, make sure to build a positive relationship with your bank, and only look at diversifying your portfolio through different lenders once you have a million dollars worth of assets with your original

CASE STUDY

I purchased a two-bedroom unit for $200,000. I received a 95% LVR loan for it, so my deposit was 5% – only $10,000. When I was looking for a lender, I was basically looking for one that would willingly lend to me at a 5% deposit. The other criteria I needed was a lender that would be OK to send out a valuer within a few weeks of purchase, as I was planning on doing renovations. Some banks force you to wait six months for a revaluation. I researched lenders prior to approaching one, and happened to get the right deal from one of the big four banks.

After I purchased the property I renovated. The renovations I wanted only cost $5000 out of my own money. I changed the painting and the tiles and left everything else as it was. I bought the property fairly cheap and once I'd fixed up the painting and tiles it was equivalent to a $250,000 property in the area. When the valuer came a few weeks later I asked for a revaluation of $250,000 and got it.

DREAM, DESIGN, DO

CHAPTER 6: RENOVATIONS

As mentioned earlier, renovations are a good strategy to quickly add value to your property. They are a major weapon in an investor's arsenal. They are also a complex issue that deserves its own chapter.

WHEN NOT TO RENOVATE

Just because you can renovate a property doesn't mean you should. There are certain circumstances where I recommend you don't renovate. Attempting to renovate under some conditions would cause you to spend money for little gain and possibly even a loss.

The first circumstance where I recommend you don't spend money on renovations is if you bought a property in relatively good condition for under market value. If you negotiated very well or, for whatever other reason, got an exceptional price under market value then there is no need to renovate. Yes, it might not be brand new and the kitchen might be ten years old – but by putting in a new kitchen you wouldn't necessarily increase the value of the property. Bottom line is, if the property is in relatively good nick, don't renovate.

In such scenarios where you don't renovate, you can probably wait six months, then go back to the bank and provide evidence (such as a dossier of similar properties in the area and their recent sale prices) that you did buy below market value, and get your property revalued at a higher estimation. That doesn't require renovations.

The other circumstance in which I recommend you don't renovate is when the market is volatile. If the market is perceived to be going down in overall capital and actual property prices are starting

money you put into the renovation might not be worth it. That's the stage where I would hold onto the property and rent it out without renovating.

WHAT TO RENOVATE

When you have a property and you've decided you will likely increase its value with a renovation, it's important to know *what* to renovate. Adding a three-storey tower with a drawbridge and moat to the back of the granny flat isn't likely to cut it.

The most important things to renovate if you're looking to improve value are the things you most notice. Imagine you're looking to buy a new house or take up tenancy in one. What would you notice on first inspection? Those are the things you should consider renovating. Inside the house this is normally the kitchen, bathroom and floors. Internal painting is also important.

Externally I might consider doing something with the walls if it will increase the visual appeal of the house. If it's a brick house and it shows the bricks I might consider rendering – which is a process of cementing over the bricks so they no longer show and the walls appear as a flat surface. If it's a weatherboard or fibreboard house, I'd consider vinyl cladding.

When it comes to external renovations, I should also mention gardening. Everyone knows a great garden adds value to a property, but I don't believe this is necessary for properties under $500,000. I'd just make sure the lawns are nicely mowed. I think landscaping a garden only increases appeal when you're revaluing more expensive properties, worth $500,000 or more.

Renovations that change the look of a house – internally and externally – are the renovations that add the greatest value. They're the items you should focus on.

YOUR ROLE IN RENOVATIONS

I see renovations as projects that need to be managed. To me,

There's no denying – project management is a lot of work and not necessarily easy. You need to have excellent organisational skills in order to coordinate everything, and the larger in scope your renovation the more it's going to take out of you. Short of hiring someone experienced (like me) to do it for you, here is the best way to go about it.

First, when you assess a project (in this case a renovation) you need to look at what your resources are. In a renovation the resources are, for example, yourself, managing the renovation. Then there are all the tradespeople involved, from plumber to electrician to carpenter to builder and so on. Then there is time, and the budget.

As you look at this renovation as a project, you want to devise an implementation plan. How are you going to best make use of your resources? You can plan this by conducting a feasibility study.

In any project management process, the first thing you do is a feasibility study. It entails a high-level analysis of what you're trying to achieve, who you're going to achieve it with, when you're going to achieve it by, and how much it's going to cost.

(Remember SMART goals from Chapter 2? Around about here would be a great time to set one!)

BUDGETING

Every renovation has a budget. The first step to budgeting is knowing what you need to budget for. Write down all the things you need to get done. The next step is working out how much you need to budget. Next to each item on your renovation to-do list set a price. This is the price you believe you should pay (or want to pay). This is your ideal target. The next step is finding tradespeople who can best fit the prices you want.

For someone new to renovating, the easiest way to go about pricing is to obtain multiple quotations from multiple tradespeople. It's very similar to finding the market value of a house; get three different quotes from three different companies for each job you

The average member of the public would normally get retail quotes, as they'll find tradespeople through one of the usual methods like the Yellow Pages or online classifieds. They don't really have relationships with these tradespeople, so will tend to pay full retail price. When you use someone with experience like me, you'll get your renovations at a much cheaper rate because I've done multiple renovations for my own properties and those of my clients. I have ongoing relationships with certain tradespeople, which ensure that the renovations I organise come with the cheapest quotes and best quality work.

Once you have a number of quotes, it's important you stick to your budget. Keep your costs as close to your target as possible. Obviously things might not go perfectly to plan, but don't fix anything that doesn't need fixing. Stick to your plan – there are things you decided to replace or fix, and that's all you need to do.

To determine what you need to replace take the above section on 'What to renovate' as a good starting point. If it's an old house that hasn't been renovated, I'd paint the house, change the kitchen and put in new floors or carpets. Then I'd put up new blinds, change the toilet, the sink, the vanity and the bathroom tiles. I wouldn't necessarily change the bathtub unless it was really bad – you could just paint over it. For the outside, if it's brick I'd render it, or vinyl clad it if it was weatherboard. Then just give the lawn a good mow.

To give you an idea, here's a list of what I would pay for each element of a renovation:

Painting (interior)	.... $3000
Painting (exterior)	.... $3000
Kitchen makeover	.... $4000
Bathroom tiling	.... $1000
Floors (carpets)	.... $2500

Floors (timber inlay) $1500

New toilet $300

New sink $300

New vanity mirror $300

Rendering $4000

Vinyl cladding $4000

New blinds $1500

Lawn mowing $200

TIMEFRAMES

The next important step to project managing your renovation is your timeframe. When do you want your renovation complete?

When I organise renovations for clients I make sure that all the tradespeople come one after the other so the timeframe for an entire renovation can just be four weeks, without the clients having to do anything.

If you want to organise your renovation project yourself, you're going to have to do something similar. That's your implementation plan.

First thing you need to know is what order you need the pieces of your renovation done. Fact is some things just need to get done first.

The next thing is, once you've selected all the tradespeople you wish to employ, make sure all these people can work at the same time. Or in a sequence. Or in stages, day one this and day two

be prepared to do a lot of juggling. Sometimes it's best to let someone else take care of project managing your renovations, as you'll save yourself a lot of headaches.

Remember, you might think a renovation going over time isn't as bad as it going over budget, but that extra time you spend renovating could be time spent earning money from a tenanted property.

KEEPING IT SIMPLE AND DUPLICABLE

Once you have a series of property renovations under your belt, one simple trick that can save you a lot of time, effort and money is to simply perform the same renovation every time.

Always doing the same set of renovations on each house you purchase means you don't have to rethink anything the next time you buy a property.

Whenever I purchase a property under $400,000, I always stick to my same 'trademark' look and feel. For the outside I normally stick to the same sort of colour scheme. For the interior I stick to similar kitchen designs and bathroom tiles. The reason I suggest this is that should there ever be an oversupply of materials from renovating a property (as is often the case), you can simply reuse those materials on your next property, saving a lot of money. It's also great because as you've done an almost identical renovation before you can simply adapt your implantation plan from earlier as opposed to coming up with a brand new one.

CASE STUDY

I found a property in Sydney's western suburbs for one of my clients early in 2013. It was severely damaged – it had graffiti all over it, it had been broken into and there were holes everywhere. I secured it at auction for $180,000, and had the total renovations quote come in at $40,000.

Many things had to be changed in the house. We had to change the

with electrical fittings, because the house had no light fittings. We had to purchase a hot water system, as there was no hot water. We had to strip the entire fibre furnishing from the outside of the house and put in vinyl cladding. We did so much that when you look at the photos it's like looking at a brand new house.

Those renovations cost $40,000, so in addition to the $180,000 the total cost of the house to my client was $220,000. After the renovations the property was revalued at $280,000.

Within a space of about six weeks that's a $60,000 increase in value in one deal. Not to mention a very happy client.

TROUBLESHOOTING

What chapter on renovations would be complete without a segment on renovation nightmares?

In my experience the biggest cause of things going wrong in renovations is when you don't account for something. It really just comes down to people not planning sufficiently.

One common nightmare is, for example, you need to get the kitchen fixed, and when you pull out the kitchen you find there's a plumbing problem. So you've got to make the call: is it important? Is it necessary I fix this problem, or can I live with it? If it's important and needs to be fixed, well that's where you need to allow some room in your budget and schedule. People often go awry when they don't provide for any budget or timeframe flexibility to account for such possibilities.

The other common nightmare is working with tradespeople. Sometimes it might happen that tradespeople don't come on time, which is usually an issue. The painters are waiting for the tiler, so now the painters are delayed. That will increase the time it takes to complete your renovation, and more time increases the time spent paying a mortgage on an untenanted property.

A good way to deal with organising tradespeople is to ask for

such the day after. Continually contact and check on their follow-through until the renovation is complete.

There is also the issue of hiring unreliable or sometimes dodgy tradespeople. The only real solution to this problem is to not hire unreliable or dodgy tradespeople in the first place!

The best way to do this is to ask around among family and friends if they know anyone who has done a great job at a great price. If none of your family or friends know of anyone the next best thing is to go on the internet and read reviews of people who have used a particular tradesperson or outfit.

When hiring tradespeople the thing you're looking for is a history of on-time work. The biggest deal is that they complete the job on time. Costs you can define a little earlier. What you want is a history of commitment. I would go so far as to recommend you call some past clients. It's like calling for employee references. I also check to see if tradespeople are insured for sufficient public liability and personal indemnity, and make sure to ask for copies of those insurances. Bottom line is, if the tradespeople you hire are good, legitimate and on time you will have no problem.

The last problem that might appear during renovations is that after you renovate there are still issues with the house. You can prepare for this possibility; you just have to make sure that the tradespeople you use are licensed and you get insured for their work. That way if there is an issue with the work done, then they're responsible for fixing it.

Finally, project managing a renovation is an exhausting process, and it's important that you're organised and up for it. There's no shame in feeling you're not up to it, as you can often save headaches and hassle by contacting someone to organise it for

If you feel that might be the case, feel free to contact me. My contact details can be found at the back of this book.

CHAPTER 7: REPEATING THE PROCESS

Once you've bought one property I'm going to assume you'll want to keep growing your portfolio. Otherwise you probably wouldn't be reading this book!

Like with many things, in property investment the hard part is starting. Once you can get past the start, you can keep rolling on towards your goal much more easily. This chapter covers how you can easily keep the ball rolling after you've made your initial property purchase. The secret is equity.

EQUITY

Simply put, **equity** is the difference between your property's market value and the total value of all loans taken out to purchase it. I define it as basically how much your property has gone up in value since you bought it.

Equity is like having virtual money. As your equity grows – through capital growth, which happens when your property goes up in value – your net worth grows. You can use this 'virtual money' to make deposits on future properties.

Equity is acquired through capital growth, but there are faster ways of obtaining it. Two of the best ways are by buying under market value and doing renovations, both covered in detail in this book. By growing your equity quickly, extracting it for another property purchase, then growing that property's equity quickly and extracting it and so on, you can turbocharge your investing journey. In a nutshell that's what I did to get my ten properties in two years.

CALCULATING EQUITY

Let's say you bought a property for $180,000. You secured a loan at a 5% deposit, so the total loan amount was $171,000. That's the amount you owe the bank.

You performed renovations on the property at a cost of $40,000, making the total cost to you $220,000. When you got the property revalued it was deemed to be worth of $280,000. Your total 'profit' so to speak is $60,000. If you were to sell your home, this is roughly the amount you would earn prior to tax.

But that's not your equity. What happens now is the worth of your home is recalculated based on the percentage of the property's cost you had to borrow. In this case it's 95%. Ninety five percent of $280,000 is $266,000.

From here you subtract the amount of money you actually owe the bank ($171,000), leaving you with $95,000. Then you subtract the amount of money you put into your renovations (because they were, after all, an expense and can't be counted as profit). In this case it's $40,000.

The remaining number, $55,000, is your equity.

This is the total amount of money you can immediately and safely extract to put forward as a deposit on a second property.

To put it as a more mathematical equation:

> *(Purchase price x Percentage of loan amount) + (Renovations/expenses) = Total cost*
>
> *Revalued property amount – Total cost = Profit*
>
> *(Revalued property amount x Percentage of loan amount) = New loan amount*
>
> *New loan amount – Renovation costs = Equity*

Your equity is not constant, however. It grows over time. Equity usually grows through one of two ways: capital growth, or paying off your mortgage. The fastest and easiest way to quickly determine how much equity a property has is to subtract the amount remaining on the property's mortgage from its current market value.

Quick equity check:

Current market value – Total mortgage amount still owing = Approximate equity

EXTRACTING EQUITY

When you go to buy a second property, you'll need a deposit and you have to pay stamp duty as well as some other upfront costs. Let's say the total you need for a deposit on your next property is $30,000. You can take that $30,000 out of the $55,000 you already have in equity, and put it into the deposit required for the second property. Simple as that.

VALUATIONS

Bank valuations are what allow you to determine your equity. You can do all the buying under market value and renovating you like, but if you don't go and get your property revalued then you'll never have a chance to create your equity.

A **valuation** is an assessment of a property's worth. There are two types of valuations – market valuations and bank valuations. A **market valuation** is an assessment of your property's value on the market, often determined by comparing it to other properties with similar characteristics in the same area. A **bank valuation** on the other hand is simply what the bank determines your property to be worth. They are often lower than market valuations, up to 10% lower, because banks want to play it safe.

In order to conduct valuations banks often outsource the task to valuers who specialise in such work. Valuers operate on behalf of the banks, and different banks use different valuers. If Bank One

B in the same suburb, so both banks do not tend to make the same valuation. As a result valuations are sometimes dependant on the day.

Let's say a strategy for acquiring $30,000 in equity is to buy a property for $200,000 and renovate it for $20,000, then get it valued at $250,000.

First you need to know the market value. In order to do so, you can use a range of tools such as <rpdata.com.au> or <APM.com.au>.

Once you have some figures, to get to that $250,000 valuation you need to perform the appropriate renovations to get the property valued accordingly, which can be approximated by comparing the finished result to properties on the market with similar criteria. As banks always value a little less than the market, it's a good idea to 'overshoot' your target. For instance, to get that $250,000 valuation, renovate with $260K in mind. Once your renovations are done, simply call up the bank and ask them for a revaluation, stating you've done renovations. From your valuation you can then determine your equity, also known as profit.

As a valuer will turn up in person to look at your property, I strongly recommend building a good relationship with them. Wherever you are in life, never underestimate the value of building relationships. I strongly advise being there when the valuer is conducting his or her valuation, and being polite, friendly and courteous. Treat them nice, because they're holding onto your money, and all it takes is a dash of paperwork for them to rid you of your profit.

Also make sure your property is in a very presentable condition for the valuation. Keep it clean, smelling nice, and make sure all the lawns are mowed.

The bottom line is, if the valuer is having a bad day, he or she might undervalue your property, and you don't want that happening.

The other thing you need to prepare for your valuation is some

that are worth (in this example) $260,000. This way you're armed with factual information when the valuation occurs, and it show the valuer you know what you're doing.

WHEN NOT TO SELL

After purchasing a property and significantly increasing its through buying under market value or renovating, you may be tempted to sell.

As an investor, I believe this is a mistake.

The first thing you need to know is that if you're selling you're not going to see all of the money you profited. Take the above example of the $220,000 property you got revalued at $280K. The $60,000 you made in 'profit' won't all come back to you. The real estate agent you sell through always takes a cut, usually at 2.5%. Then you'll have to pay capital gains tax, which is a tax applied by the Australian Government on any profits made on the disposal of any asset. Capital gains tax varies from property to property. Add all of this up and you haven't got $60,000 anymore.

The other thing you need to consider should you really be thinking of selling your investment property is what are you going to do with the money? Are you going to go on a holiday? Fund a startup business? Reinvest it?

If your answer was 'reinvest it', then you might as well not sell. I would instead recommend you take the equity out of your property and use it to fund a second property. Now you have two houses and you're adding more value to your portfolio as opposed to getting rid of the first house to buy the second.

If you have a property worth $280,000 and you're going to buy another property at $280,000 then you'll have $560,000 in assets. Property appreciates at roughly 6 to 7% per year, so you'll have $560,000 appreciating at 6 to 7% as opposed to $280,000 appreciating at 6 to 7%.

CASE STUDY

My whole property investment journey is a case study on repeating the process. I bought well with my initial property (the details of which can be found in Chapter 1) and from there extracted the equity to put forth for another property.

I employed strategies such as buying low and renovating to make sure I always made money on the way in, giving me a chunk of equity to play with after each property purchase. I would then always put my equity towards another property purchase. The details of my strategy are expanded in Chapter 4. Essentially this is how I built my portfolio of ten properties in two years.

Sure, this may sound easy, but at times it wasn't. The point is that I kept going when it got tough and I eventually got to where I am today.

TROUBLESHOOTING

A number of things can go awry that might stop you from repeating the process and turning one investment property into a portfolio.

The first of these is if your property gets undervalued by the bank.

Say that $250,000 property you renovated for $20,000 only got valued at $270,000, causing you to have made zero profit, and giving you zero equity to play with.

You could dispute the valuation with the bank, and call in the evidence of renovations and similar properties in the area with your target market value. It's a good idea to find three examples of similar properties in the area to present. But provided you've done your homework, made the property presentable and were friendly and courteous to the valuer, there's no reason why they shouldn't give you the right answer.

The second problem that can stall your investment journey is when the bank declines your loan application because you're borrowing to pay it back. This is the reason why you should always look to buy properties that are cash-flow positive: essentially positively or neutrally geared. When the property is not costing you money and you don't have to dig into your income or savings to maintain it the bank is much more likely to lend you more money.

The last thing that can commonly stall a person's property investment journey is loss of motivation. Unlike the first two reasons, which are caused by external factors, this problem lies entirely within a person. The only real way to get past it is knowing what your true motivation is and following that and that alone. For more about finding your true motivation please refer again to Chapter 2 and the exercise included in it.

If you know and are in touch with your true, deepest motivation and continually refer your actions back to it, you should have no problem remaining motivated on your investment journey.

DREAM, DESIGN, DO

CHAPTER 8: LEARNING FROM THOSE WHO'VE SUCCEEDED BEFORE YOU

Like I said at the very start of this book, investing in property is a journey. But sometimes journeys can go a little off track. You might find yourself at a point where it's hard to keep going.

If you're looking to make this journey as easy on yourself as possible, such that you can reach the goal you've set, this is the chapter for you.

MY NUMBER ONE TIP

They say failure is the best teacher. I completely agree. That said, failure in the property game can hurt. I'm sure everyone who's looked into property investing has heard a tale of someone financially crippled by a bad investment, a tale passed around like some campfire ghost story. I always urge people not to be afraid of failure, but when failure means owing a couple hundred thousand dollars you have a very practical reason to be cautious.

Luckily, there is a very elegant solution – nobody ever said it had to be your own failure you learn from.

And just like you can learn from other people's failures, you can learn from their successes. This is even more important. If one person can achieve success at something, so can you. My number one tip for the aspiring property investor is this:

Learn from those who've succeeded before you.

Property investing is a vast journey and there is plenty for other

If you approach every person and situation with the mindset of *'What can I learn from them/this?'* then you will go far.

Learning doesn't just stop at investing though. You can go much further than that, and actually *learn* to be successful. In anything you choose to be successful in. Winning is universal.

The truth is it's all in your head. People who are successful have particular mindsets, particular ways of thinking. Once you learn how they think and begin to think like them, you too can become successful, whether in property investing, business, relationships, sport, crocodile wrangling, or whatever else.

YOUR SURROUNDING INFLUENCES

So if the best way to learn to be successful is to learn from those who succeeded before you, what is the best way to actually learn from them?

The answer is to have them in your environment. Surround yourself as best you can with them. Find the people who already have the results you want in your life and attend their seminars, read their books, become their friend and invite them out for coffee.

The simple fact of life is that we are the people we hang around. We are our influences. Why do you think so many smokers have friends who are also smokers? Or why successful crime novelists often admit to reading lots of crime novels? Or for that matter why rich and successful people often hang out with other rich and successful people? The reason is because like attracts like.

The fastest way to change anything about ourselves is simply to change the environment we're in. By removing or introducing something to our environment we open ourselves to change. For example, if you want to quit smoking, quitting will be easier if you stop hanging around other smokers or places you associate with smoking. Likewise if you're thinking of starting a business, the best thing to do is hang around successful entrepreneurs.

ways of doing things will slowly influence us until eventually we begin to think just like them.

You may be thinking to yourself right now, *'But where do I find them?'* To absorb the success mentality you want, here is what I think you should consider.

BOOKS

The first thing I recommend is reading more books. Not just any books, but rather those kinds of books that will help you become a better person.

In my experience the books you read are indicative of the life you live. In essence, you are what you read. Just like you absorb the vibes and opinions of the people you hang out with, you do the same with books. And television for that matter. So I recommend reading a personal growth book or an investment book for at least fifteen minutes a day, every day.

It's vital to have an understanding of your mind and of human potential, and how to get out of your own way so that you can make room for change. I would normally say that whatever you have in your life already is what you truly deserve – that's why you have it. So if you want anything more in life, you actually have to change some ingredient to be able to have what you don't. By changing the books you read you will love yourself for letting your mind expand, because you'll tap into the brains of highly successful people who have done what you want to do. For $20 they can be in your brain every day talking to you.

What's more, if you're not surrounded by a society that's encouraging or aligned with your goals, positive books will help keep your mind positive and directed towards the outcomes you want in life.

Even If you are indeed one of the lucky ones, surrounded by positivity and encouragement, you won't always be surrounded so. You'll still be affected by the ins and outs of life. You'll still get

Make reading positive, empowering books a habit. Just like you make sure you take fifteen minutes out of a day to have a shower (or at least I hope you do!), take fifteen minutes out for a book too.

RECOMMENDED READING

The first book I recommend you read is **How to Win Friends and Influence People by Dale Carnegie**. You may have heard of this book, as it's a classic from 1930 and a foundation stone of modern personal development. Don't let any of that turn you off however; every word in it rings as true today as when it was first published. I recommend this book more than any other.

How to Win Friends and Influence People teaches you about relationships. Even though we've been talking about property and money and investment strategy, if you look behind it all you'll come to see everything is relationships – the relationship you have with your bank, your mortgage broker, your plumber and your valuer. Every time you interact with someone you're forming or developing your relationship with them. Understanding how relationships work is very important to your success, and that's the reason I recommended you read this book. And when I say 'success' I don't just mean as a property investor. I mean in any area of life where you have to deal with other people.

The second book I recommend is **Think and Grow Rich by Napoleon Hill**, which is also a personal development classic. This book deals with the mentality around success, and attempts to create a formula for success that anyone can follow. By interviewing more than 500 highly successful people of the time, including heavyweights like Henry Ford and Franklin Roosevelt, author Napoleon Hill analysed the commonalities in their belief systems and formed a road map one can follow to adopt their thinking patterns. It's a fascinating read by itself, but the main reason I recommend it is because it allows you to get inside truly successful people's heads so you too can adopt the way they think.

The third book I recommend is **The Magic of Thinking Big by**

we have to dream big. And if we dream big we have to do big things.

Many people have big dreams that remain exactly that, dreams, because when they wake up they do nothing about them. A dream that doesn't turn into action remains a dream forever. When a dream turns into reality it's because you've actually done something to make that dream happen.

The Magic of Thinking Big opens your mind to ideas and pictures of what you really want to be doing with your life and how you really want to be living. It then empowers you to take the actions that go with your dreams and fight to make them come alive.

In terms of investing and understanding money I recommend **Rich Dad Poor Dad by Robert Kiyosaki.** The reason I recommend this book is simple – if you're an employee or a small-business owner (which is approximately ninety percent of the population) – this is a great way to understand the mentality of the rich. Have you ever wondered why is it that ten percent of the world owns ninety percent of the wealth and ninety percent of the world works for ten percent of the wealth? By reading that book you'll understand that the people in the ten percent who run the world think very differently from the rest. They see life differently and even speak differently.

For example, an employee or small-business owner normally talks in the language of **'This is how much I earn'** as opposed to an entrepreneur or highly successful investor who says **'This is how much I'm worth'.** That is a very different outlook to life. The mindset of the rich and successful is vital to understand if you're looking to join their ranks!

The final book I recommend is more on the spiritual side: **The Power of Now by Eckhart Tolle.** If you're not OK with who you are as a person, as a human being – no matter what you do, how much money you make or how successful or influential you become – it all means nothing. You're probably going to go to bed feeling unhappy regardless, so you might as well not bother.

If you're not happy, you're just going to find more reasons to make more money and continue to just – be. You'll think that next investment or big wad of cash you make will bring you the happiness you want, but when it doesn't you'll think it's the one after that. That's the cycle. I recommend this book so that you understand more of who you are as a person, where you are in life, and come to be at peace with that. It's worth more than any investment portfolio on the planet.

SEMINARS

The next thing I suggest is that you attend a personal development or investment seminar at least once a month, for a period of one or two hours minimum.

There are two reasons. First, you'll be in an environment where you can learn face to face once a month. Most likely it will be a group environment, which is great because in a group the energy is so much higher. You'll automatically be stimulated and ready to take more action. The other important reason is you're surrounded by like-minded people who aspire to get better, and so you're changing your environment.

A word of caution though: not all seminars are the same. Personal development is an unregulated industry where almost anybody can just front up and call themselves a motivational speaker. I have known motivational speakers and 'life coaches' who are dynamic, engaging and insightful on stage, but emotionally unstable wrecks in their private lives. That's why I recommend you do your research on the speaker you're going to see prior to attending their seminar.

Find seminars conducted by people who have achieved the results they advertise and are honestly living by those results. What I want to know is what that person does when *not* in the seminar, not what he or she is doing during it. Emotional stability is also a big green tick. If you find those people, the seminars they host are worth every cent of the ticket price.

MENTORING AND COACHING

I feel you have two choices in life. Either you can learn the hard way and try to figure it out all on your own, or you can find somebody else who has figured it already and learn from them. And you can do that directly. Not only will your teacher become one of your surrounding influences, they'll be directly changing you.

I'm the sort of person who would rather be taught and learn from someone else who has succeeded, and that's why I've always paid to be coached and mentored in certain different areas of life; including property investing, relationships and spirituality. Others get professional training in other areas of life such as health, cooking and hobbies such as scuba diving.

Scuba diving makes for a great example actually. If you wanted to go scuba diving, would you just buy all the equipment and jump straight in the water? Or would you rather go and get trained by a professional prior to dipping your fins? For me, that's an easy choice.

Actually there's a law behind why you have to get trained and certified to do scuba – because otherwise you'd probably die. Which is fine with me. But just because you're not going to die immediately and horribly in property investing, that doesn't mean 'dying' slowly and horribly by going bankrupt as you try to figure things out on your own is OK.

That's why I always recommend mentoring and coaching, so that there's someone to hold you accountable to what you're doing. Someone who has a plan and a proven system and all you have to do is follow the steps. You might make your own system out of it and maybe modify it and improve it like I have always done, but I've originally always started with somebody else's plan. Because they're bigger than me, they think bigger than me, and it's likely they've taught me to reach higher than I could have on my own.

OUTSOURCING

The last thing I want to touch on is outsourcing. Outsourcing is a mindset of the rich and successful that you might as well adopt

When it comes to an employee or small-business mentality, it's all about trading time for money. It's the **'I have to do it all'** sort of thing. A small business does the accounting, cleaning, selling, marketing and everything else because it's a small business. The flip side is an entrepreneurial or large business; for example a big bank, insurance company or telecommunications company. They have large numbers of employees, and they're all doing the work for a certain few people who own a large amount of shares in the company – the Board of Directors. Everything is outsourced. All the stuff required for the upkeep of the business is handled by someone else. Even if you look at a bank, it might outsource its IT, telecommunications, marketing and PR – just to focus on its core purpose, which is lending money.

This is something to think about as an investor. Because that's what you are. You have to say **'My job is only to invest and make money and create wealth. My job is not to paint the carpet or fix the roof, my job is to find those people. My job isn't to find the best loan; that's my mortgage broker's job. My job is not to understand legal contracts; that's my lawyer's job.'** And so on.

The same should be applied to managing your properties. You're an investor, and property management is a job for a property manager. It's not your job to be a private landlord and have to deal with headaches at two in the morning because the hot water pipe broke. Wouldn't you much rather pay someone to do that for you? Of course you would. Hire a property manager so that you can focus on the area you're great at: investing.

Once you begin to understand the concept of outsourcing, which can include mentor figures as well, then your investment journey can truly begin.

CASE STUDY

It was attending a motivational seminar for the first time that opened my eyes to the way I could be living. It was where I first found inspiration and courage to take the initial steps towards they life I now lead.

I found a vision of the life I wanted to lead, and had a true, honest understanding of my motivations for doing so. Skip forward ten or so years and here I am, living the life I dreamed of.

Everything I have done, everything I have achieved, could not have been possible without the people who taught me, mentored me and educated me along the way. I am truly grateful to every one of them.

You can't do this alone.

TROUBLESHOOTING

Sometimes it happens that a person just loses motivation. It can happen for a variety of reasons, which include being put off by the amount of effort required, boredom, or having something new and shiny come along.

Whatever the reason, if you find yourself losing motivation, always go back to the exercise in Chapter 2, the **one hundred reasons why**. Do it again and again if you have to. It'll give you reason to keep moving forwards if you ever begin questioning yourself.

Once you have your true motivation, it's just a matter of keeping on going. You'll feel immensely rewarded when you achieve the results you desire.

AFTERWORD

DREAM, DESIGN, DO!

Although I've given you the basics and a good strategy to follow, there's far more to property investing than what we've just covered. With some of it the only way you're going to learn is by jumping into the water yourself. And with some of it you may want to have some help. If there is anything I can do to help you're welcome to call my office any time.

I wish you all the best in making your dreams come true. Your own journey is just beginning, and I hope to see you somewhere along the path.

If you'd like to get started in property investing I can be contacted at:
<www.dreamdesignproperty.com.au>.

Zaki Ameer
November 2013

DREAM DESIGN
P R O P E R T Y
CREATING WEALTH THROUGH PROPERTY

JOIN OUR GROWING FACEBOOK COMMUNITY OF 18,000 FANS

 www.facebook.com/dreamdesigndo

QR CODE TAKES YOU TO
DREAMDESIGNPROPERTY.COM.AU

DREAM, DESIGN, DO

NOTES

NOTES

DREAM, DESIGN, DO

NOTES

DREAM, DESIGN, DO

NOTES

DREAM, DESIGN, DO

NOTES

DREAM, DESIGN, DO

NOTES

DREAM, DESIGN, DO

NOTES

DREAM, DESIGN, DO

NOTES

DREAM, DESIGN, DO

NOTES

www.ingramcontent.com/pod-product-compliance
Lightning Source LLC
Chambersburg PA
CBHW051812170526
45167CB00005B/1987